INSTINCT FOR FREEDOM

INSTINCT FOR FREEDOM

A MAVERICK'S GUIDE TO SPIRITUAL REVOLUTION

ALAN CLEMENTS

NEW WORLD LIBRARY
NOVATO, CALIFORNIA

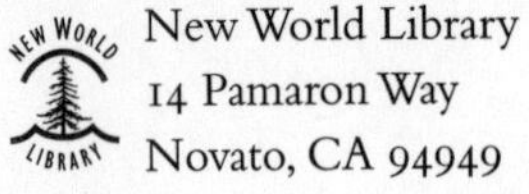

New World Library
14 Pamaron Way
Novato, CA 94949

Cover design by Mary Ann Casler
Typography by Tona Pearce Myers

Library of Congress Cataloging-in-Publication Data
Clements, Alan, 1951–
Instinct for freedom : a maverick's guide to spiritual revolution / Alan Clements.
p. cm.
Includes index.
ISBN 1-57731-212-0 (hard cover : alk. paper)
ISBN 1-57731-539-1 (paperback : alk. paper)
1. Liberty—Religious aspects—Buddhism. 2. Spiritual life—Buddhism. 3. Human rights—Religious aspects—Buddhism. 4. Buddhism and politics—Burma. I. Title.
BQ4570.F7 C54 2002
294.3´444—dc21 2002007503

First paperback printing, April 2006
ISBN-10: 1-57731-539-1
ISBN-13: 978-1-57731-539-1
Printed in Canada on acid-free, partially recycled paper

New World Library is a proud member of the Green Press Initiative.

Distributed by Publishers Group West

10 9 8 7 6 5 4 3 2 1

Dedicated to

My loving parents, Warren and Linda Clements

The people of Burma, in their revolution of the spirit:
A struggle for freedom, democracy, and human rights

And the future of life and freedom on earth

If you assume that there's no hope,
you guarantee that there will be no hope.
If you assume that there is an instinct for freedom,
that there are opportunities to change things,
there's a chance you may contribute to making a better world.
That's your choice.

— Noam Chomsky

CONTENTS

PART TWO
Consciousness, Meditation, and the Great Unknown 89

PART THREE

World Dharma — Liberation through Living

Three passions, simple but overwhelmingly strong,
have governed my life: the longing for love,
the search for knowledge,
and unbearable pity for the suffering of humankind.

— Bertrand Russell

INTRODUCTION

If we're lucky, every now and again, we have a decisive encounter — an event that changes the course of our lives, forever. With logic and comfort thrown to the wind, we set out on a new, more invigorated trajectory, unleashing our passion and vision upon the world. Such moments are glorious and gorgeous, mysterious and tormenting. They contort us, bend us — squeeze out every vestige of pretense, compromise, and inauthenticity. Some call this magic. Others call it synchronicity. Some may even call it madness. It has all those elements, and more. I call these moments, taken together, the Dharma life — a response to our instinct for freedom, the natural urge of the heart to know itself and seek its liberation from all obstacles, real or imagined. This revolution of the soul demands that you no longer deny your true calling. It demands that you find your higher love, which then helps you reach beyond whatever is holding you back.

But this awakening requires something of us. We must pay a price: we must fall in love. To take liberation as our life's purpose is the greatest of challenges. It means making the terrible beautiful and kissing each heartbreak as divinity itself. Mother Teresa encourages us: "For love to be real, it must cost. It must hurt. It must empty us of Self."

One of my earliest encounters with this form of love happened during my first journey into the war-torn jungles of northern Burma. It was a moment that touched my heart, inspiring me to seek a new, higher understanding of freedom — unconfined by dogma, superstition, or religion.

One evening I was speaking with a dignified twenty-nine-year-old Burmese woman, a university graduate who had fled her home after the pro-democracy uprisings of 1988. As we sat under the night sky, with a candle burning between us, we discussed the principle of nonviolence: How can it be effective against a totalitarian regime that tortures and kills unarmed civilians? At what point is self-defense necessary, if only to survive?

In the near distance we could hear soft guitar music and the voices of students singing love songs, which they did every night. Groups of students would gather and walk with guitars, stopping at the huts of resting fellow students. As we listened to the music, I spontaneously asked my companion if she'd ever been in love. She paused for some time and regarded me evenly. Her dark brown eyes twinkled in the firelight. "Yes, I have been in love," she replied. "Two and a half years ago my fiancé and I were to have been married. We loved each other deeply. We'd known each other from childhood. But the demonstrations in 1988 began only two weeks before our wedding. It was an incredible moment. We so desperately wanted freedom and democracy. The time had come when we thought it would be possible to come out from under the boot of military oppression that had trampled us since we were children.

"First we went out and marched. The next day my sister and brothers came out with us. The following day my mother and father came out, then my aunts and uncles, until my whole family was in the streets. Suddenly, from nowhere, the soldiers appeared. They grouped together in three long rows, their automatic weapons and bayonets aimed at us.

"We in turn, many thousands of us, knelt down in front of the soldiers. We sang to them, 'We love you; you are our brothers.

All we want is freedom. You are the people's army; come to our side. All we want is democracy.'

"But they had orders to fire, and they did. Many students, some friends, and some of my family members were shot dead on the spot. We had no idea that our own people would kill us. I could scarcely believe it was happening. I was terrified. There was blood and screaming everywhere. The cracking of gunfire echoed as everyone panicked and ran for cover. People began falling down — a young friend of mine died in my arms. I looked for my family. They were gone. My fiancé and I began to run.

"We went on running for the next two weeks, deeper and deeper into the jungle. I was still with my fiancé, along with a dozen other students, and we miraculously managed to evade the soldiers. Sometimes we had to bury ourselves under leaves, cling to the banks of rivers, or stand rigidly behind trees as soldiers passed by.

"We felt like animals being hunted, sleeping sporadically on the forest floor. It was cold and unbearably painful. We were constantly bitten by ants and mosquitoes. Yet we managed to stay alive.

"After two weeks of running, nearing exhaustion, we all contracted malaria. We were extremely weak, feverish, and nauseated. That night the soldiers ambushed us. It was to have been the day of our marriage — instead, my fiancé and I were separated during the firefight.

"I have never seen or heard from him since that night. I don't know if he's alive or not. I dare not contact his family or my family, because it would put them in great danger if the regime found out."

We sat without stirring. The candle flickered in a momentary breeze and time seemed suspended. "I still think about him," she said. "I do miss him sometimes. But being out here in the jungle for these past few years, living under the tyranny, my values have changed. I'm in love with freedom. And even if I'm caught and tortured to death, if it will help restore freedom in my country, and freedom in the world, I will die in love.

"Yes, I have been in love," she said softly. "And I remain in love."

We stared at each other for a long few minutes. She broke the silence saying, "Freedom is a choice. Isn't it? As is love."

Coming to terms with our true function as humans requires a dedication to fulfilling a dream. Inevitably, this takes us from ordinary comforts and private concerns and thrusts us down a wild existential highway few dare to travel willingly. Not only will the Dharma life — the way of freedom — break our contracts with conditionality, exposing how we grasp and brace and hold back, it will confront the entire apparatus of avoidance — every fear, every complicity, every nuance of self-deception. Breaking free from the gravitational force of a fear-driven presence, we re-inspire our courage again and again, until we truly understand that our dignity is our greatest worth and that our instinctual intelligence is the natural wisdom that will guide us in finding liberation through living.

What I'm talking about should not be confused with transcendence, or an attempt to escape one's self or the world. This way of being has nothing to do with life-denying attitudes. Nor am I proposing a return to a "primordial beingness" as the only true means by which to overcome human suffering. This freedom is not fear driven but life giving — it includes the flesh, the ordinary self, the sacred and mundane as one. It's about making life our art.

The Dharma life is born out of realizing our essential interrelatedness: we cannot live without each other. This means *feeling* more than just one's own self-interest, or the interests of one's family. Defining ourselves as tribes and nations is in large part why we are teetering on self-extinction. We must really understand our inherent inseparableness. The more we do, the more we'll feel the joys and the sorrows of others as our own.

Seeking one's own liberation alone is outdated thinking. In the opening scene of the film *Crouching Tiger, Hidden Dragon* the hero makes this point beautifully. He is asked by the woman who secretly loves him why he left the solitude of the monastery and reentered the world. In a slow, measured tone he says, "My enlightenment did not have any bliss associated with it. It felt something more like despair, but greater. It was such an immense sorrow that I could not take it. I could not go on. It was saying... return to reality."

Embracing the Dharma life and responding to our instinct for freedom illuminates reality, not just our opinion of it. As falseness is revealed, we must continuously realign ourselves to the truth. Being guided by intuitive intelligence, which often defies adequate explanation, usually means entering the jaws of raw, tumultuous existence.

The Dharma life is a daily reawakening to explore and map the Mystery. Turning our lives into an epic adventure, we blaze our own trails, even if it means defying social mores or breaking taboos that attempt to suppress and control our impulses.

This revolution will not be won or lost in a meditation retreat, a city street, a living room, or a monastery alone. It will happen on the front lines of the human heart — that stormy region where good and evil, genius and madness, peace and war battle for dominion over conscience, freedom, and love. When compromise, doubt, or hesitation no longer hold appeal, it is my belief that you will inevitably encounter a glimpse of the holy unexpected. You will begin listening to your instinct for freedom — what you really love — and leave the rest behind.

Here is how it happened for me.

PART ONE

THE STRUGGLE FOR FREEDOM

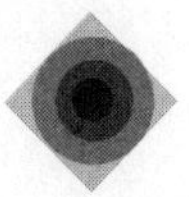

SEEKING THE SOURCE OF SUFFERING

In 1970, when I embarked on this journey, I assumed that genuine spiritual development was only cultivated through years of vigorous training under the guidance of a qualified Dharma teacher. Years later, at age twenty-nine, this belief took me to an isolated monastery in Rangoon, Burma, where I practiced silent meditation up to twenty hours a day for many years during the seventies and eighties.

This first phase of my Dharma life — my decision to leave the world and enter intensive meditation — was neither predictable nor easy. On the contrary, it was mysterious and troubling! It came on slowly, as a whisper of discontent, and crested into an existential crisis. At the time I was in my second year at the University of Virginia in Charlottesville, where I studied prelaw and art history. Somehow I felt a deep dissatisfaction. I was restless and weary, struggling to make sense of my life. Outside I saw a planet in flames — consumed with war, vengeance, and suffering. The truth was I hated school and hated the American government for waging a senseless war in Vietnam. I felt that my education was just a euphemism for indoctrination — programming me to find satisfaction somewhere within the machinery of mediocrity and domination. Besides feeling manipulated, I also feared that if I continued to pursue my studies with the intention of becoming a lawyer, I'd find myself somewhere down the road successful and forgetful, and somehow call it happiness. Almost everywhere I looked people seemed automated — living comfortable, predictable lives, held together by propaganda and lies. When I turned my attention back on myself I felt the torment of my own self-deceit. But the problem was, I didn't know how to untangle myself from the web of complicity.

As my anguish peaked, I resolved to get to the bottom of it. Actually, my life started to take on a strange, organic momentum of its own. My torment had an entelechy — a driving intuitive wisdom that seemed much larger than logic. One afternoon, I said, "Enough!" I drove to my favorite spot an hour away — a lookout high in the Blue Ridge Mountains. I parked and trekked through the snow to an isolated ledge with a majestic view of the Shenandoah Valley. I sat down in the freezing December night and entered the jagged, confused claustrophobia that had been confining me for the previous year. I had to know what my life was about — my passion and my purpose — and whether I had the courage to live it.

I remember that night so well. I trembled, cried, and quaked. Eventually, I could take no more. Standing up, I screamed at whomever and whatever this sick god was who was driving the show — "Why so much madness, horror, and pain?" The anguish cut through my heart like a knife. It scared me that I understood that resolution wasn't simply an issue of changing environments, settling somewhere on a piece of beautiful land, being more creative, having more money, or finding another relationship. Nor did it feel like a psychological question. It frightened me even more to feel that I had played out what the world had to offer, and any resolution had to come from within. The fire to resolve the crisis burned deep in my core. This was my first dark night of the soul.

I stayed on the mountain throughout the night — talking to

myself, pacing back and forth on the ledge, smoking cigarettes, and becoming clearer and more confident by the hour. I didn't have answers to the big questions but things became unmistakably transparent — my life was a lie and I had to make a change, fast.

At sunrise I drove back to Charlottesville, packed my belongings, went to the dean of the college, relinquished my scholarship, and withdrew from school. By that afternoon I was cruising home, stoned and in bliss, en route to my girlfriend's apartment in Virginia Beach.

Soon after, I began pursuing my true passion — art. Painting had been something I had done since childhood and now without the pressures of school looming over my head I was free to create, to plumb the depths of my interior. I was primarily drawn to abstract and surrealist art, where I found ample room for life reflection. The images became my metaphorical fantasy world, a place I would go to soothe my soul. My paintings symbolized an uncensored, spontaneous life — a life I wanted to live but to which I had no real access.

Progressively, I went further out in my art. I began regularly painting under the influence of hallucinogens. This became my existential therapy, my Dharma — a vehicle to explore consciousness. By consecrating the substances, I used them to probe the more hidden, complex areas of my being — those contradictions and peculiarities that lurk beneath the skin of everyone, as well as the personas that protect them. But no matter how deeply I would go, I couldn't shake a troubling sadness. My urgency was amplified by an aching inner emptiness and a haunting perception of mortality. No person or thing could assuage my anguish and awareness of death.

A TURNING AWAY FROM THE WORLD

By 1974, three years after I left school, I descended into my second dark night of the soul. I was sitting in front of a painting I had just completed. I called it "mechanical man — a self-portrait." It was a group of four robotic-looking figures. Their faces were without features. They were entangled together and dependent on each other, unable to stand alone. They were framed within a box-shaped world — a cubed myopia imprisoned by perception. My mind felt like that cubed myopia — a prisoner of itself. Entranced in a societal hypnosis, I felt mechanical. Everything felt out of my control and I desperately desired a freedom from the known — my box-shaped world.

In a moment of epiphany I realized the obvious — I needed assistance. I couldn't do this on my own! I wanted a guide, a wise friend — someone who understood the nature of the mind and who could help me to understand the mystery world behind my eyes. But whom could I turn to?

Miraculously, days later, while washing my clothes in a Laundromat in West Palm Beach, Florida — the city where I had moved to be near a warm ocean as I pursued painting full-time — I was scanning the bulletin board when I noticed a flyer. It was an advertisement for the Naropa Institute — the first university in America devoted to the study of consciousness, started by the Tibetan Buddhist Chögyam Trungpa Rinpoche, in Boulder, Colorado. It was the subtitle that grabbed me. It said something like, "Explore your mind. . . . Discover the Dharma . . . . Be free."

My girlfriend Catherine and I picked up and drove to Boulder. After a provocative summer at Naropa, having learned the basics in Buddhist meditation, we decided to go overland to India as the next phase of our spiritual journey. But it was only upon arriving in Burma — an ancient South Asian Buddhist culture, with its five thousand or so monasteries scattered throughout a land the size of Texas — that I felt I had found what I was looking for. The elegance of the people, their generosity and grace, and their extraordinary devotion to the teachings of the Buddha touched me like nothing else I had ever known. I had absolutely no desire to leave. It became important to me to study with the elders of the Theravada Buddhist tradition, the banner-holders of traditional Buddhism and insight, or *vipassana,* meditation. At the time only seven-day visas were available for foreign visitors. It wasn't until much later that I discovered the country was also a totalitarian terror state ruled by General Ne Win — an eccentric, xenophobic, and ruthless dictator.

After nearly two years in Asia — kicking around Buddhist monasteries, tropical beaches and meditation centers, exhausted and broke — I returned to America looking for some direction on what to do. Deciding that I wanted to pursue my life as an artist, I moved to Los Angeles. The contrast to silent monasteries and the simplicity of Asia was overwhelming. Within weeks my ambitions crumbled into the simple struggle for survival. I tried to stabilize by painting more. But nothing worked.

Early in 1978 I hit rock bottom. One evening, midway through a painting, something snapped. I broke my paintbrush in half. Threw my paints out. Cut up my canvases. The whole art thing felt masturbatory. I threw out my Dharma books. They were useless. You couldn't find freedom in a word any more than you could lick ink to liberate yourself. I went out on the balcony of my home in the Hollywood Hills and looked out over a sea of illuminated city blocks, contemplating my next move. I flashed back on my last LSD trip, just months before on an island off the coast of southern Thailand. The experience had implanted itself in the marrow of my soul. I thought if I relived it I might find the key to what I was looking for. I needed to find a reason to *be,* fast. At the time the experience in Thailand left me feeling that all I wanted to do for the rest of my life was be in silence and meditate, to vanquish the core suffering that was embedded in my chest. So why was I in L.A.?

My acid trip had one theme: hell, literally and metaphorically. It was a twelve-hour descent into anguish. I remember coming away from it thinking how *radically right* the Buddha was in seeing how the very structure of consciousness was flawed. Everything was conditioned and interdependent. Every perception was in flux. Everything was in time. Our faces. Our hearts. Nothing lasts. Life was a sand castle constantly eroded by limitless time. We were dream creatures on a canvas of photons, solidified by deluded minds. Happiness was a bargain with ignorance, sealed with denial.

I heard the Buddha speak to me that day: "Long have you suffered in this samsara — life after life. During this endless cycle of rebirth and death you have cried more tears than the waters in the four great oceans. Have you not suffered long enough to turn away from existence? What more do you need to see? What other form of pleasure do you need, before you seek the wisdom of transcendent escape?"

It would be this one dogma that drove me into the monastery: understanding that the source of suffering — namely greed, anger, and delusion — is inside oneself, and understanding that by removing these conditions, suffering ceases. Why seek refuge in anything external? As the Buddha said, "By oneself alone is one defiled, by oneself alone is one purified. Seek your own salvation with diligence."

I remember the epiphany I had on that balcony in L.A. that night. It would be the awakening that would send me halfway around the world to save my soul. I felt that I had come to the end of seeking. I was done with books. Done with open-ended travel. Done with yet another aimless conversation. I was done with psychedelics. I was done with feeling self-pity. I was done pretending that I would find happiness in the outer world. Freedom had to come from within. I wanted to know the same silence that all saints throughout history had spoken about as the essence of the human experience. Sitting still in meditation, closing my eyes, and going inward with a sustained self-awareness were the only logical things left to do. I wanted enlightenment. I wanted perfect peace, a perfect realization, a perfect transcendence of my suffering self and this burning world.

FORM IS USEFUL BUT AWARENESS LIBERATES

I chose to be ordained as a monk by Mahasi Sayadaw, an elderly Burmese Buddhist meditation master, who was then visiting New York City. I had met him briefly during my first trip to Burma two years prior. The day after my ordination I flew to Burma, along with Mahasi Sayadaw and several other monks.

When I arrived in Rangoon I had no idea what was in store for me. I had been given a "monastic visa" and, as it turned out, was the first American allowed to actually live in a Burmese monastery since the military coup d'état in 1962. Except for short visits, mostly limited to twenty-four hours, few Westerners, other than diplomats, had spent any extended time in Burma. This was uncharted territory. It was a great leap of faith. I was a kid maverick in many ways, a brash renegade artist with a rebellious nature, conditioned by psychoactive substances, rock 'n' roll, existential art, and a love of sex and freedom.

I plunged into an alien world. I shaved my head, renounced food after noon, became celibate, and lived with teachers I didn't know, with little support from friends or family. After an initial period of intense struggle, living as a monk began to sparkle with beauty. I found myself in a world where people spoke to the matters of my heart. They provided a setting where meditation could be practiced on a full-time, open-ended basis. They provided everything necessary — shelter, food, medicine, robes — all given with love and kindness. The Dharma teachings were shared in the same way, openly and freely. I had finally found an environment that met my own intense questioning with guides who challenged me to my depths.

The first teacher was Mahasi Sayadaw. He was a magnificent man who inspired a fascination in me to explore human consciousness as fully as possible. He also taught me about dignity and the courage it takes to sustain freedom. Sayadaw U Javana was my first meditation instructor in Burma, and he grounded me in the basics of how to objectively observe the mind. Sayadaw U Sujata, who embodied great warmth and humor coupled with the outrageous, supported me in not being so frightened of myself. Sayadaw U Pandita was to become my spiritual father, brother, mentor, and best friend. I had never known such a provocative and stimulating relationship. He brought out the best I had, and he enjoyed chiseling away at the rest.

These Dharma guides, or "spiritual friends," as they are traditionally called, expressed extremely refined human values. In my relationship with Sayadaw U Pandita, I faced for the first time in my life the issues of honor and surrender. He demanded complete honesty and surrender to *reality,* not my opinion of it. He initiated me in how to conscientiously interrelate to others and myself. He also opened me to the expansiveness of what intensive awareness meditation practice could offer. He was a great spiritual friend.

As time went on, and as I became more fluent in meditation, a wonderful sense of nurturance grew in me. I had never felt more content in my life. At times, I literally wept with joy at having found my tribe, my family, my purpose. I felt blessed, as though I were riding a sacred vehicle into the great unknown. My experience seemed timeless. It was from this profound and complex period of my life that I learned what spiritual practice can truly mean. The second section of this book is devoted to an "inside look" at the actual process of how intensive insight meditation transforms consciousness.

Yet, all things change. After years of training and living in the monastery my circumstances shifted drastically. Although I had done nothing to provoke them, in the early eighties I was forced to leave the monastery because the Burmese government was unwilling to renew my visa. After two days of agonizing reflection, I decided to disrobe as a monk. A few hours later, wearing jeans, a T-shirt, and sandals, with just a few dollars in my pocket, I flew to Bangkok, took a train south, and eventually arrived at an isolated bungalow on an island in the South China Sea.

Not long after I arrived on the island, I was invited to teach a ten-day meditation retreat by the Thai abbot of a local monastery. At the end of it I received a donation that was just enough to buy a one-way ticket to Los Angeles. Days later I reluctantly returned to the West.

The reentry was maddening. It was a confrontation with everything I hoped to avoid, namely my life. No amount of spiritual training could have prepared me. Immediately, I felt the aloneness, the separation, the frivolity of society. The onslaught on my senses was overwhelming, the technological hum deafening. It was all moving so fast and felt so harsh.

The monastery held a deep sense of protection, quiet, and simplicity. I never faced a choice of what to wear; it was always the same robes, the same color. There were no telephones to answer, no flights, no driving, no parties, no cooking, no sex, no movies. It was always the same schedule, day after day: meditating, studying, and discussing the Dharma, year after year. Almost everyone shared a refined alliance of purpose. It was my intimate spiritual family, a close-knit community of radical seekers.

In America's altered reality, the distance and struggle in most peoples' eyes saddened me. Everyone seemed preoccupied with money, security, and diversion. Life felt consuming. I too began to feel these pulls. Few people seemed to have much time for their hearts' higher calling, or even for themselves. I had no idea how sensitive I had become as a monk.

So I concentrated on connecting with friends, and I also began to lead meditation retreats. This gave me great joy and eased the transition tremendously. I loved being around spiritual explorers, people genuinely striving to know themselves more fully. In fact, in some ways this period was a continuation of my time in the monastery — but without the safety of the monastic form. I was just another human in the great sea of life. It was as if I were stripped of all protection. I felt naked. There was just my human consciousness manifesting right in front of me.

In coming back, I felt I was cast into a situation where I was my own guide. I would now have to provide all the encouragement and kindness my teachers used to supply. I kept hearing Sayadaw U Pandita's final words to me the day I disrobed: "Trust that the seeds of purification are within you. Nurture them and you will awaken. The form is useful, but it is awareness that liberates."

Entering the next phase of my journey, I began realizing that *life experience* was my greatest teacher, and therefore the highest vehicle for spiritual awakening. This led to an understanding that the Dharma — finding liberation through living — was not a doctrine to memorize and subsequently practice. Rather it was a metaphor for freedom itself, a "Dharma intelligence" that functioned to release inhibition and fear while opening the heart to wisdom and compassion.

THE EYES OF THE ENEMY

Transforming my own understanding of the Dharma from doctrine into metaphor was long and complex. Although the process began soon after I disrobed in 1983, it was not until 1990 that it really evolved. I remember having just finished leading a meditation retreat in Australia and picking up a copy of *Time* magazine with the cover story "Bullets in Alms Bowls." The military regime in Burma had raided hundreds of monasteries in Rangoon and Mandalay, arresting many monks and killing others, based on the maniacal fantasy that the Sangha — the Buddhist clergy — was attempting to overthrow the dictatorship.

Since Burma was my spiritual home, I responded, I think, as any loyal son or daughter would to their own family. The monks and nuns were my Dharma parents; they nurtured me in ways I had never known before. With Burma's future in jeopardy, I shuddered at the possibility that the Buddha's teachings would be silenced. My fears were not far-fetched. The Buddhist cultures once found in Afghanistan, Pakistan, and India had been decimated by Mogul invaders. Buddhism in Vietnam and Laos had been devastated by Chinese-backed Communism. In Cambodia, Buddhism had been almost completely destroyed during Pol Pot's reign of terror. And in Tibet the Chinese had been annihilating Buddhist culture since their invasion in 1949. Who could say how long Burma would last?

I immediately decided that I would return to Burma in an attempt to support my spiritual family in one of its darkest hours. A few days later, when I got to Bangkok, I learned that the military authorities had closed Burma — sealing the population in and closing foreigners and journalists out — turning this ancient, mystical country into a totalitarian nightmare, what the BBC would call a "land of forty million hostages."

Through underground contacts, I clandestinely entered the country. Nothing could have prepared me for what I saw. When I first arrived in the jungle to join the resistance, it all appeared to be quite simple. Like many unsuspecting noncombatants, I was immediately taken in by the vast hillsides of shimmering golden poppies. The steep mountain peaks shrouded in mist beckoned thoughts of romance and beauty. Clear jungle streams cascaded into large waterfalls and on into deep pools. It was not long, however, before I would see this land without the pleasant tourist's gaze. The regime was liquidating Burma's rural population. Within days of landing in the jungle I saw thousands of terrorized refugees fleeing from Burmese government soldiers. Boy cannibals in camouflage trained as headhunters — maddened on hate propaganda and saturated with cheap alcohol and drugs — ravaged the countryside with orders from the dictators in Rangoon to exterminate *en masse*. Burma had become blood-soaked; it was being mercilessly torn apart.

Villages were smoldering, mortared into charred ruins. And among the ruins, massacres — My Lai–style. Severed heads, still blindfolded. Even the dogs had been killed, blackened to a crisp like pigs at a luau. Everywhere I went I saw wailing mothers running, exhausted and starving, clutching their children. Some of the children were dead, mangled unrecognizably by land mines disguised as toys. I heard tales of brutal gang rapes by soldiers that went on for days and months.

At one point, I was with my Burmese guides, hunkered down on a ridgeline deep in the jungle. Suddenly, over the camp radio, the movements of troops loyal to the dictatorship were intercepted. "North 100 meters," the student with the headset yelled out. His words were like razors, severing me from the insulation of tomorrow. We lowered ourselves deeper into the earthen trenches. AK-47s were unlocked and ready to fire. An hour passed.

"Shit," Maung Win blurted out under his breath. "We can't just sit here and wait... we've got to find them." He nodded to the others to get ready to move. He turned to me and asked solemnly, "Coming or staying?"

His eyes were unblinking. Mine were frozen.

Maung Win and I weren't strangers. In fact, we were old friends. We'd been Buddhist monks together in Rangoon, back in 1981. My few weeks in the jungle with him had been deeply unsettling. Simply put, I thought Maung Win was an affront to all that I considered spiritually correct.

Calculated savagery was nothing I had ever known. Initially I resisted, trying to mask the pain by rekindling spiritual beliefs. But even compassion felt like a glib cliché — a dogmatic shield that had nothing to do with my true feelings. Everything I thought and said reeked of rhetoric. As time in the jungle expanded my reality, I was to learn that there comes a time when spiritual aspirations and pacifist ideals cease to have meaning. One is willing to kill for freedom.

Just the day before we had been snaking through the jungle together. My arrogant judgments must have been apparent. I was disdainful of Maung Win for taking up weapons to fight the regime. After all, Aung San Suu Kyi — the leader of Burma's struggle for freedom — was advocating nonviolence as the best means of political change.

Suddenly Maung Win turned around and began shouting in my face like an irate sergeant. With each tirade he pushed me backwards. "I'm sick of your judgment. We live under dictatorship. Do you know what that means? Haven't you seen enough?

"Imagine not having your passport stuffed in your pocket. You can leave anytime, and go sit in a retreat — as if you know what freedom means. You're an idealist."

I stood unmoving and speechless, not knowing what to think. Where *did* I stand?

"Listen" he said, cutting me off from reflection. "I couldn't justify sitting in meditation while my brothers and sisters were being killed. Our teachers taught us to love even those who hate us. But try to love with a gun pointed at your head.

"After they tortured my brother, I disrobed and joined the resistance. My heart is with my people, not with my enlightenment."

"There are other ways than weapons and war," I said, with a small shred of defiance.

Maung Win became outraged. He thrust his AK-47 in my chest and pushed me backwards, shouting, "What if it was your girlfriend who was raped? What would you do? Sit back and be mindful? Become a dead Buddhist?"

He turned around and walked away.

I followed in silence. Inside I felt like broken glass.

Back at the camp, Maung Win made my decision for me and asked me to stay behind and look after a member of the group who had just become ill with malaria. He and the four others jumped from the trench and went out to find the enemy soldiers before they found us.

That night Maung Win was killed in a firefight. The other students returned to camp with a captured soldier. They believed he was the one who had actually shot Maung Win. While the others slept, I was put on guard duty, asked to keep an eye on the enemy soldier.

We sat upright staring at each other. His hands were tied. A small fire separated us. I had a pistol pointed at him, with instructions to "shoot if he stands up or yells." The gun was warm and damp from the sweat of my hand. I felt splintered with rage and disoriented with a terrible sorrow. My mind oscillated between two thoughts: "How easy it would be to shoot this guy" and "Am I prepared to die?" Both thoughts were repulsive.

I looked down the barrel of the gun into the sad eyes of the soldier. "Can I ask you a question?" he asked. I nodded in affirmation.

"Would you tell me... why are you risking your life for my country?"

It was a good question. I tried to enter his mind, to find his motivation. Was it a trick? Why did he want to know? I hesitated, saying, "I'll let you know." He nodded his acceptance and we went back to staring at each other. As time passed I noticed that our breaths were alarmingly synchronized. This observation further eroded the distance between me and the enemy.

Was this a ploy? Had he been trained in escape? My suspicion tightened my finger on the trigger. He remained unflinchingly fixed on my eyes. They were cold and penetrating but strangely human too.

His question forced me to think the unthinkable. Why was I sitting in a free-fire zone with a pistol pointed at this soldier's head? Was I crazy? There was something truly absurd about it all. The question took me back to the beginning — to my earliest contact with Buddhism and the reason why it had seemed to make so much sense.

BURNING IN A WORLD ON FIRE

It was 1966. I was fifteen years old and it was the first night home after two weeks in the hospital recovering from a car accident. I had been driving home after a party in my parents' new Chevy, having just got my license the week before. I was drunk. My friends and I drank every weekend. We weren't especially rowdy. We just smoked, drank, and had fun with girls. That night, as I was driving, I lost control at forty-five miles an hour and hit a telephone pole head-on. My head went through the windshield. I had to have two operations and hundreds of stitches to close the eighteen inches of jagged lacerations and a scalp pushed back to the crown. The surgeon told me I was lucky to be alive. At the time I wasn't so sure.

In arriving home I looked like a mummy from the neck up. My head was wrapped in gauze with openings for my mouth, nose, and ears. My eyes were swollen shut. The headaches I had after the accident were monstrous and unremitting. I became opiate-dependent.

I felt nauseous and terrified. Days before, my mom had asked the doctor the hard question, "What will he look like?" I gulped, waiting for the answer. They thought I was asleep under the bandages. The doctor whispered his answer, "He won't look the same. But it's his brain we're concerned about. We don't know how severe the trauma is."

I think this was the source of the original shame that I felt about the accident. I was certain I had ruined my life. And I knew my carelessness had become a terrible burden on my family.

Each sip of soup that first night home was a chore. The sound of the television in the living room offered a muted comfort, distracting me from my self-hatred. My brother Dave's presence also eased the pain. He was five years my senior and home for the night from military academy.

I remember the news coming on, hearing the distinctive voice of Walter Cronkite. He was telling us, yet again, about those killed and injured in Vietnam. As I listened I could sense a mounting tension in the room. Then my mother gasped.

"What's happening?" I asked, knowing something was up. "Tell me." When no one answered, I turned in my chair and pried open an eye to look at the screen myself. Cronkite told the story of a Buddhist monk who walked to a city square in Saigon, sat down, crossed his legs, doused himself with kerosene, lit a match, and set himself on fire. His act of self-immolation was intended to draw attention to the victims of the war. His gesture symbolized the suffering of his people.

I was awed. How was it possible for him to sit still while his body burned? The idea was totally alien and at the same time strangely familiar. I just sat there with an eye pried open, transfixed by the miracle and the madness of what I was seeing. The power of that famous image seared itself on my mind.

After the news my brother got up, walked to the bathroom, and closed the door. I knew he was upset. We all feared that he'd get drafted after graduation in the summer. Death loomed large in everyone's mind. No one wanted the war. Even my dad, a retired chief petty officer in the navy, was against it.

I got up and went to the bathroom, where I found my brother sitting on the edge of the tub. Dave's head was in his hands. I sat down and tried to comfort him by rubbing his back. I loved him. He was my brother — my security, my guidance, and my hope.

After a few minutes of silently sitting together, Dave whispered in my ear with a strong and loving voice, "You want to take a look in the mirror?" His invitation sent a shiver up my spine. I refused. He said it again. After several more refusals and an equal number of convincing comments, he came back with the clincher, "I have to leave soon and won't be home again for a few weeks. Now is as good as it gets." I agreed, hesitatingly.

I was shaking so much Dave had to help me up. I stood in front of the mirror feeling broken. For as long as I could remember I had been attacking every surface imperfection with militancy. Nothing went unjudged: my skin, my teeth, my hair. The color, size, shape, and length of everything was manipulated or repressed — anything that didn't conform with the "right image." The mirror was me; it was how I knew myself. It never lied. I braced myself as Dave asked, "You ready?"

"Do it," I replied.

Once Dave had unwound the gauze I pried open my eye again. I knew it would look bad but nothing could have prepared me for what I saw in the mirror. I collapsed. Not only was I the ugliest human I'd ever seen, I realized those massive, grotesque scars would remain, a symbol of my stupidity, for life. I was so angry at myself I wanted to die. But something that night saved me from my darker self. The anger turned to rage and the rage carried with it the sheer force of determination. I flashed on an image of that burning Buddhist monk. I saw him reflected in the mirror. How could I transcend my body? How could I transcend pain? What inner reserves did he draw on in choosing a noble death? I entered the projection of his burning body and pledged, "I want to know what you know." This became the driving metaphor that fueled my idea of the spiritual journey.

TAKING RESPONSIBILITY FOR ONE'S MIND

Thirteen years after my car accident, in 1979, I landed in Burma as a Buddhist monk on a quest to find the inner fortitude I had seen displayed by the Vietnamese monk so many years before.

I stepped out of the plane onto the ramp, following behind a procession of elderly Burmese monks. At the head of the procession was my Dharma teacher, Mahasi Sayadaw. In front of us, on the tarmac, thousands of devotees were seated, holding candles. As we walked from the plane to the terminal, the throngs began chanting an ancient Buddhist Pali verse. I had learned it from the translator just days before. It was the Metta Sutta — the Buddha's teachings on loving-kindness. Over and over again they chanted, "May all beings be free of harm and danger. May all beings live in peace and freedom." I thought I had arrived in heaven, a mystical realm beyond anything recognizable to my life on earth. I'd never felt such beauty or seen such devotion. It filled me with love, transporting me beyond the tormenting inner fires that had been consuming me for as long as I could remember.

Once in the car we were chauffeured the seven miles from the airport to the monastery. The road was lined with thousands of additional well-wishers, packed so tightly there was barely room for the car to inch its way through. I was stunned. People were everywhere — on rooftops, in the trees, on balconies, in storefronts and windows — poised to catch a glimpse of the country's most revered meditation master as he returned from his only Dharma teaching trip to the West.

As we drove I reflected on what it was about Mahasi Sayadaw that had stirred me to follow him to Burma. To me, he was an archetype for uncompromising spiritual commitment, inspiring me to seek the highest freedom possible. I had never had anyone encourage me in that way. As a meditation master he devoted his life to the exploration of human consciousness. He was renowned throughout Asia for both his depth and his dexterity in navigating enhanced states of mind. His skill as a meditation master had inspired hundreds of Dharma centers worldwide and he was widely considered to be one of the world's foremost Buddhist scholars. He was also a prolific author, writing seventy-five books exploring the nature of consciousness and the overcoming of human suffering.

Once we arrived at the monastery I was shown to my room and told to begin my meditation retreat. The next morning I arose at the scheduled 3 A.M. And began a series of one-hour sitting meditations interspersed with one-hour walking meditations. Except for a short breakfast at 5 A.M. And lunch at 10, the day was in silence. We practiced self-awareness twenty hours a day, until retiring to sleep at 11 P.M.

After the first few days of my retreat the honeymoon was over. Every meditation became an hour-long struggle. I struggled with the constant desire to escape the physical pain, restlessness, and relentless schedule. It was the most difficult undertaking of my life. I wanted to run away, but I couldn't because there was no place left to go. I had to stop and face myself.

Mahasi Sayadaw always made it sound easy. All he asked me to do was to follow the schedule and when I sat in meditation to "watch my breath . . . be aware of the changing physical sensations in the area of my chest and abdomen as the breath enters the body and when it exits the body. And whenever your awareness wanders from this task . . . whether thinking, planning, daydreaming, judging, or anything else that enters your stream of consciousness — be aware of it. Once noticed, gently bring your awareness back to the primary object of the breathing processes — either the breath coming into the body, or it leaving the body. Do this over and over. That's all."

By the fifth day I felt like a caged animal. I wanted to be everywhere other than my breath or my mind. Ironically, I felt awake and present in my day-to-day life in America. As an artist I would often paint for many hours at a stretch, feeling both blissful and totally refreshed. But the opposite was true in meditation. Without an external task I was unable to "be present" with any degree of proficiency. My mind wandered everywhere.

As the twenty-hour days stretched on I found myself judging anything and everything I could get my awareness on, both inside and outside. Nothing remained unscathed. Up to this time I had never thought of myself as either judgmental or angry. There, however, in the sanctity of one of the most revered Buddhist meditation centers in the world, I was projecting aggravation everywhere — blaming anything, animate or inanimate, for instigating my misery.

I was angry that we weren't allowed to sit on cushions in the meditation hall, but had to sit on thin cane mats instead. I was angry the windows weren't screened to keep out the flies during the day and the mosquitoes at night. I was angry that dozens of mangy dogs were allowed to live in the monastery — barking and fighting and fornicating day and night. I was angry the center was built in the middle of city, where we were forced to listen to the loud music blaring over the public speakers in the neighborhoods surrounding us.

To make matters worse, when I went to see Mahasi Sayadaw

for my scheduled interviews, he would ask me to describe my meditation practice. I told him that I was observing an inordinate amount of judgment and frustration. To this he would simply reply, "please continue and you'll progress."

This angered me even more. I even started to think that his answers were contrived and brief so as to avoid further angering the already angry American. I shuffled him into my repertoire of "reasons for rage."

As the days inched on this cycle of anger fed itself. I began to notice ever-greater details of what was wrong about life in the monastery and how the American monk could correct it. My mission went from self-discovery to CEO. I wanted to change everything. And as my desire increased, the problems grew. The dogs barked louder. They fornicated longer. They became mangier. I even devised a plan to take up a "mutt relocation fund" and build a shelter for them at the back end of the monastery. When I brought it up to Mahasi Sayadaw he didn't seem interested.

My upset made the schedule feel longer. I could have sworn the clocks became slower, making the one-hour sittings even longer than an hour. I was amazed at what the mind can do to invent distraction and sources of anger.

Then the food came under attack. It was too oily. Too much meat. Not enough leafy greens. Then the weather was never right. It was too hot one day. Too rainy the next. I started to think that I should have postponed my trip and come during the winter months, not during monsoon season. Then the bed was too hard. The water too cold. The mosquitoes bit harder and deeper. Their bites itched longer. The knee pain spread to the back and then the neck, then all three places at once.

Just when I thought it couldn't get worse it did. The monastery work crew started building a new meditation hall adjacent to ours! "Why?" I demanded. "This one isn't even filled." Tell the workers not to talk. Why were they allowed to smoke?

On and on and on . . . I judged and became more and more angry. I remember sitting down in meditation determined to get to the bottom of this problem once and for all. Soon after closing my eyes I heard a faint growling sound from just outside my window. How unusual I thought. I went outside and to my surprise I found a litter of puppies under the tree in the leaves. They were adorable. When I looked closer I saw that their eyes had not yet opened. They were growling because they couldn't find a nipple to suck. How interesting, I mused. These newborn creatures were angry, too.

For the next few days, with their eyes still unopened, their growling intensified. As it did, my own anger subsided. I began to realize the folly of projecting blame onto apparent causes external to myself. I had been scapegoating *life* with my primordial anger. Those puppies came into the world predisposed to anger. As I did. As we all did. Ignorance was innate to the operating system.

In this way, I began to understand that ignorance and a host of other self-generated emotional realities started long before the monastery deprived me of "my happiness." This was also one of my first insights into the futility of thinking I could resolve the suffering that arose in the present by attacking the past for the "real cause." It helped me to restrain from pathologizing aspects of being and defused the tendency toward blame, judgment, and retaliation.

When I told Mahasi Sayadaw the story, he said, "As long as there is anger in the mind it will find a reason to assert itself. You are here to awaken by taking full responsibility for your mind as the source of your feelings. In Burma we say, "Blame never ceases by blame. Anger never ceases by anger. Only by love do they cease. This is an ancient principle." "Please," he concluded with eyes soft with compassion, "trace your judgments to their source — your own mind — and there you will find resolution and peace."

It was at this point, three weeks into my retreat, that I began to appreciate just how bound we are as humans by conditions not of our own making. By birth, complexity and confusion cannot be avoided. They are conditions innate to every human. I understood ignorance to mean partial clarity or, in some cases, a pure blindness to reality. Of course, with ignorance, errors in judgment are inevitable. If ignorance arises with other mental states, such as anger or judgment, one often creates an imagined reality and then projects blame on it, thus scapegoating a phantom that doesn't actually exist. This is what I had been doing. Mahasi Sayadaw later said that "ignorance is a type of mental hallucination."

To highlight this point he told me a story about a wealthy Burmese woman in the late 1800s who had never seen the ocean. Being landlocked her whole life she decided she would go on a boat in the Andaman Sea. So enthralled was she by the magnificent colors of the water, that she paid the captain a fair sum of money to pull the boat into a lagoon harboring dozens of shades of blue and green sea. Once anchored the woman began collecting the different colors of seawater in tiny blue bottles. Apparently, she wanted samples so she could import them back to her area of the country and increase her fortunes. When she returned home and poured them out for her friends, she was shocked to see that each bottle contained the same clear water.

In this way I began to understand how terribly misleading it can be projecting "inherentness" or "absoluteness" into perceived experiences. It's the difference between living in illusion and living in reality. In theory, the notion of mental projection is easy to understand, but in the heat of the moment, where passions and attachments often run deep, it is a challenging obstacle to penetrate and overcome, requiring nothing less than total responsibility for the self-generated state of one's own mind.

THE HEART OF DARKNESS

Back at the fireside in the Burmese jungle, I looked once again at the enemy soldier. Again, I thought about his question, "Why are you risking your life for my country?" I began to feel more trusting and intimate toward him. Maybe he feared *his* death, I thought. After all, he was human, like me. At the same time something primal in me fought back. He killed my friend. He's destroying the country I love. I felt myself squeezing the gun more tightly. I could sense that he felt my anger. We just sat there looking at each other, feeling. It was an amazing moment, especially when I saw a tear run down his cheek.

As we sat in silence, a part of me still wanted to harm him. But as I reflected both on his crime and the collective stupidity he was a part of, I asked myself, "Where did this darkness come from?" Was there, in fact, intrinsic evil? Did we all fight — an archetypal repository of demonic energy, which at any moment could spew hell and oppression through the unmindful crevices of our psyches? Was there a Manson, a Hitler, a terrorist in *everyone,* which could be triggered by unforeseen circumstances? And if so, I pondered, from where does this wickedness arise? From sexual repression? Humankind's irrational drive for domination and power? A tortured childhood? A blueprint from birth? From the genetics of our reptilian past? Or was it karma — an ancient action contorting one's behavior? Or are we in a cold universe without true meaning? Why do humans have hearts with darkness?

Whatever the source, the conditions are clear. Suffering exists! And human beings for one reason or another perpetuate the torment with enormous fervor and conviction. Am I exempt, I wondered to myself? Am I beyond the possibility of an act of violence that from another perspective is an "act of evil?" With these thoughts in my mind I gazed more closely at the Burmese soldier. He wasn't as cold as I had initially observed. He looked shaken. His lower lip began to quiver. I wondered if he was married. Did he have children? I imagined their anguish as they learned that their father had been captured, or had died.

As I reflected further another layer of separation between "me and him" peeled back, and as it did it exposed some of my vulnerability. The line blurred even further. I began thinking that I may not be able to shoot him after all if he were to yell or try to make a run for it. This scared me. Lives were in danger. Suddenly I went with my instincts. They told me to recognize our shared humanity. I took the risk and lowered the gun and finally responded to his question, saying, "I was once a Buddhist monk in your country. It was the gift of the Dharma that brought me to Burma. Your country is my spiritual home. It gave me my first taste of inner freedom."

He looked at me for a few seconds. His large brown eyes were deeply saddened and welling with tears. "I was once a monk, too," he said.

Was this true, I wondered. Or was it a ploy? After a long pause he asked, "Would you take the photo from my back pocket?" I aimed the pistol at him again and gripped it more tightly, fearing that at any second he would try to steal it. Our eyes locked, unblinking. Trust was the final obstacle between us.

As I felt the pounding of my heart I realized I couldn't bear the thought of him shooting my sleeping comrades and me, too. It would be wrong of me — completely dumb. But I had to know if he was telling the truth. I wanted to believe him. So I leaned over, keeping the pistol pointed at his head, and pulled the photograph from his pocket. Bringing it in close to the embers of the fire, we both looked down at it. It was true. There he was — a Buddhist monk in robes and a shaven head, sitting with his eyes closed in meditation. He looked up at me and me at him. We entered each other's eyes and hearts. I felt him for one brief second as my brother.

Doubtless, there is evil in this world. How and why are beyond any of us to know. What we do know is that the human heart is not sectioned off into black-and-white regions of pure good and absolute bad. We are not living in a world with only two kinds of people: the right ones, us, and the wrong ones, them. Alexsandr Solzhenitsyn, Russia's Nobel laureate, said, "If only it were all so simple. If only there were evil people somewhere insidiously committing evil deeds, and it were necessary only to separate them from the rest of us and destroy them. But the line dividing good and evil cuts through the heart of every human being. And who is willing to destroy a piece of his own heart?"

"I must make the most of this moment," I thought to myself. "There are four types of persons in this world," my teachers in Burma would say. "There are individuals who succumb to the forces of darkness, inside and out. Others who run from them. Still others who speak of confronting them. And there are those who engage these forces in battle — at all costs — even till death if need be." So be it! I recommitted myself to looking deeper into my own heart of darkness, that mysterious region of my own being, and said yes! Yes, I accept you. With your fears. With all of it. I want to know you. I want to learn to love you. I will meet this challenge!

THE QUEST FOR GREATER AUTHENTICITY

It might seem obvious, but it took me some time to realize that it's one thing to speak about spiritual qualities, such as wisdom, compassion, and freedom, in the safe and sanctified context of a Dharma retreat, with an audience of silent and good-hearted people, while it's another thing altogether to manifest those qualities in more complex circumstances. When you lead retreats all the time, as I was doing, you can become rather insulated in your so-called depth — your own insights and realizations. You speak about love, forgiveness, and liberation, but these words fall short of expanding one's heart, say, to include the harsh realities of living under a dictatorship, or holding a malnourished infant in a resettlement center filled with ten thousand other hungry people, or comforting a terrified young girl who has been raped. These words strain under the weight of looking into the eyes of a captured enemy soldier who just killed your friend with a bullet to the head, or understanding the suffering of a screaming child who has just lost his parents to sniper fire.

Soon after my return from Burma in 1991, I stopped leading meditation retreats, gave up the lease on my home, sold my few belongings, and embarked on an open-ended sabbatical with almost no money. I was thirty-nine years old. I felt I needed more life experience to discover the authenticity and the compassion missing in my spiritual understanding.

A few years later I was based in Paris, making a living as an author, screenwriter, and journalist. My prime interest was examining the psychology of genocide, nonviolent revolution, and the courage of the oppressed. To do this required also exploring the mind of totalitarian regimes — past and present — including Burma, Romania, the Czech Republic, and Serbia, whose dictatorial regimes at the time attempted to shape their citizens into a faceless, dull sameness, where creativity, critical analysis, and even the slightest whisper of dissent were fiercely repressed. This work brought me in touch with a number of dissident writers and thinkers, some known and famous, others anonymous and on the street.

I began to study the writings of Noam Chomsky, who has brilliantly articulated in such books as *Necessary Illusions: Thought Control in Democratic Societies* how the powers that be use misinformation and propaganda to "manufacture consent," whereby one is unknowingly manipulated into believing lies that function to support the needs of the elite. This led me into a study of indoctrination. I noticed that on a much more subtle level the same "programming" occurred in many spiritual scenes, including Buddhism. Dogma was mistaken for Dharma and self-deception was considered self-realization. Examining why some people feel that it's better to believe and belong than to authentically quest at one's edge became a fascinating new area of discovery.

Before visiting the war zones of Burma and, later, the former Yugoslavia, I had assumed that I had some real relationship to freedom. It took the intensity of these experiences to teach me how contextual and myopic "my freedom" actually was. Take away my comfort, my security, my clothes, my home, and leave me witness to ethnic cleansing, and I realized that my liberation was relative indeed. In addition, I thought that I had a reasonable understanding of generosity, until I saw people sacrifice their lives to save others. I thought I understood compassion until I had a stranger shield my body with his from the shrapnel of a rocket attack. These experiences and many others shook my spiritual identity, cracking my persona of self-certainty open further.

Although living in the former Yugoslavia during the final year of the war was one of the most disturbing periods of my life, it was also one of the most beautiful. I had been invited there in 1994 by my dear friend Marcia Jacobs, who was a senior officer for the United Nations' refugee agency for Bosnia-Herzegovina. When the conflict was over, I would often return to Zagreb and Sarajevo to visit friends. I love Croatia and Bosnia. The people I came to know have remarkable passion, humor, and brilliance. Groups of us would often stay up well past dawn, in smoky, candle-lit underground cafés, jazz bars, and nightclubs, drinking coffee or sipping brandy or beer, talking about love, existentialism, or the politics of genocide. These discussions were fed by seeing firsthand humankind's cruel urge to annihilate its own species in the name of God, ideology, nationality, religion, or any number of other perversities masquerading as truth.

Although I was shaken and depressed after my glimpse of genocide in the jungles of Burma, by the time the war ended in the former Yugoslavia my soul was on fire — burning in existential turmoil beyond anything I had known. By the fifth year into my sabbatical, while documenting the atrocities of war and revolution, I had cried thousands of tears. Even with antidepressants I often felt like my heart could still burst at any moment. This darkness was to kindle a new spark of light and meaning.

LET'S DANCE!

There inevitably comes a point when the weight of holding up unnatural self-images becomes a burden. It is a time when you begin to feel the fraudulence and hypocrisy of being someone other than yourself, as clichéd as that may sound. One of the first things I learned living in conditions of tyranny — and yet one of the hardest lessons to actually practice — was to simply feel, listen, and love, in order to support those who were suffering, without being so arrogant as to try to heal or fix them. To keep this truth close to my heart I would often recall to myself the story of an Aboriginal woman. When approached by a white social worker, who said, rather presumptuously, "I'm here to help you. What can I do?" the Aboriginal woman replied, "If you are here to help me, please go. But if you see that my freedom and yours are linked, then please stay and we can serve each other."

To feel the "linkage of our freedom" is perhaps the greatest lesson we must learn to ensure our survival. This point took on powerful meaning during one of my sojourns into Bosnia. It was in the spring of 1996, several months after President Clinton had ordered NATO planes to strike Serbian positions around Sarajevo, which after only twelve days of bombing, ended three-and-a-half years of horror and the death of 250,000 people.

On one visit to Sarajevo, I was having a glass of wine with a friend at an outdoor café in the city's main square. Marina, like many others from the former Yugoslavia, was from a mixed ethnic-religious background. Her mother was a Croatian Catholic and her father a Serbian Orthodox.

Marina and her younger sister survived the forty-four-month siege of Sarajevo primarily by huddling with their parents in their kitchen. The kitchen was the most protected room in their two-bedroom flat, which was situated in a blown-out high-rise adjacent to "sniper alley." She and her family, as with everyone else in Sarajevo, faced many hardships, including living without electricity, running water, and heat through frigid high-mountain winters, and surviving on porridge, grass, nettles, and flour. Marina's struggle was to intensify, however, when both of her parents were diagnosed with cancer. After three years, and without medical treatment, they passed away within a few months of each other.

On that day, Marina had invited me to accompany her to the cemetery to pay respects to her deceased parents. It was to be her first visit to the gravesite since her mother had passed away. I considered her invitation both a gift and an honor. For Marina life centered around her family, and although deceased, to be introduced to them was something sacred to her — a sign of dear friendship. I also knew that Marina's mother had been her best friend. I wanted to support her.

Mostly, I stood in the background watching my friend sanctify the space with her grace and her sensitive silence. I kept her company while she washed her parents' headstones, placed fresh flowers on their graves, lit candles, recited poetry, and otherwise sat silently in prayer.

At one point I turned away and, looking out over the cemetery — a sea of tombstones and grave markers — I noticed how the cemetery was divided into three distinct sections, each divided by a different color of headstone.

When I asked Marina about it she explained how each of the three different ethnicities and religions in her country had their own area within the cemetery. White marble headstones were for Muslims, black for Catholics, and gray for Orthodox. Since the cemetery was ruled by segregation, her mother and father were buried in different sections. We acknowledged the absurdity of the situation with a sad, silent shrug.

As Marina turned back and faced her mother's grave, I was propelled inward by a memory from a few days earlier. I was driving back to Sarajevo from Srebrenica, the town where several thousand Bosnian Muslims were slaughtered. My friend Marcia Jacobs, who had since left her job with the UN and was now working for the International Rescue Committee, accompanied me. After hours driving through bombed-out villages, we stopped by the side of the road to take a break. In a nearby field some men were digging. We walked over and found a mass grave — a pit of putrefying human flesh. It was heart-wrenching and frightening. We gasped from the stench.

But this wasn't anything new, I reflected. The human world is fraught with murderous expressions of ethnocentricity, xenophobia, and nationalism. The twentieth century has been witness to obscene brutality. Stalin. The Holocaust. Hiroshima. The genocides in Timor and Rwanda. Pinochet's terror in Chile. Pol Pot's sea of cracked skulls in Cambodia. The death squads of Guatemala. Saddam Hussein's massacre of the Kurds. The crushing of democracy in Burma and Tiananmen Square. The hanging of Ken Saro-Wiwa in Nigeria. In the name of what? Truth? Freedom? Nationalism? Globalization? Christ? Allah? Oil? God?

I came back to the present with my eyes focused on the grave. Protruding from the ground, I noticed an exposed hand with a ring on one of the fingers, glistening in the sunlight. I stared at the ring for a long time. There was no way of telling whether it was a man or woman, but the ring spoke about a kind of marriage — a bond of love — not just to another, but to God, to life and liberation beyond racism, tribalism, and all lethal fantasies. It symbolized a marriage to the world, to the Dharma — the journey of liberation from fear and illusion — and to a deep discovery of whatever principles govern this terrifying and beautiful existence, which is so sick, so mysterious, and so gorgeous, too. For me the ring also symbolized, as any good marriage would, a radical commitment to know the heart — oneself — as much as humanly possible.

At that moment, I realized that no matter what I knew or how free I assumed myself to be, I had a hell of a lot more room for wisdom to grow. I asked if it were even possible to rectify the archetypal split of good and evil in one's own heart. Could I transcend love and hatred, right and wrong, this world and nirvana?

Standing before a mass grave made the notion of spiritual transcendence seem preposterous and inhuman. The Dharma — finding liberation through living — was a means to embody our humanness, not to nullify it. It was here that a major shift in my Dharma understanding occurred: entering my humanness with a respect for the indivisibility of freedom was infinitely more important than pursuing the projected perfection of transcending duality and coming to the so-called end of my own personal suffering. Yet it had been these latter goals that had been principally driving me for the previous twenty-five years of spiritual life.

The realization stayed with me throughout the night, seeping in much more deeply than any meditative insight I had ever known. The following day I absorbed it even more thoroughly. I had been accompanying a doctor friend of mine on her rounds, visiting patients in a clinic on the outskirts of Sarajevo. Many of them were still speechless from their traumas. Others cried uncontrollably. One young boy was lying on his bed squeezing a small teddy bear, curled up, motionless. He was no more than nine years old. A woman sat next to him and dabbed at his tears with a handkerchief. She would then dab her own tears. My friend raised the sheet covering the boy's lower body. He had no legs. She then covered his lower body again, kissed him on the cheek, and said something in Bosnian to the woman, who I assumed was his mother. The situation was too much. I excused myself and walked outside. What would it take, I asked myself, for us to use our hands not to harm each other, but to touch each other kindly — to rub each other's backs, and hold each other's hands? What type of consciousness was needed to turn off the killing machine, and reawaken the soul to its natural beauty? Was this an idealistic dream?

As I thought more about it I recalled a conference in southern California where I had been invited to lead insight meditation back in 1989. The conference was on Buddhism and psychotherapy and was headlined by the Dalai Lama of Tibet, who had just received the Nobel Peace Prize for his efforts to end the Chinese occupation of his country — and bring light to one of this century's greatest tragedies.

At one point in the conference the Dalai Lama told a story of a fellow Buddhist monk in his homeland whom he greatly admired. The Dalai Lama explained that this monk, known as the "Weeper," was given his name because he was so attuned to the suffering of others that he often wept. The Dalai Lama was deeply inspired by the Weeper's highly developed compassion.

Of course, crying all the time does not describe your stereotypical well-adjusted Buddhist. In fact, in most spiritual circles such a person would likely be evaluated as severely traumatized, in denial of some dysfunction, and very likely prescribed antidepressants. If the condition persisted, as it did with the Weeper, it's possible the person would be committed to a psychiatric hospital and medicated even further. Yet somehow this weeping monk was an inspiration to the Dalai Lama himself.

I had always been deeply touched by this story, but in this

context it took on mythic proportions. How does the human heart open to such an extent that it *feels* the inherent linkage of love and freedom among us all? What wisdom would awaken a deeper engagement not just with our immediate relationships but with the interrelatedness of all life? I reflected on the notion of *ubuntu,* a word rooted in South African culture, meaning, "A person *becomes human* through other persons." Archbishop Desmond Tutu describes *ubuntu* as the opposite of "I think, therefore I am." In other words, my humanness is inextricably bound up in yours. Such a person, he says, "does not feel threatened that others are able and good, for he or she has a proper self-assurance that comes from knowing that he or she belongs in a greater whole, and is diminished when others are humiliated or diminished, when others are tortured or oppressed, or treated as if they were less than who they are." He concludes, "What dehumanizes you, inexorably dehumanizes me. And what elevates you, elevates me."

Returning to where I stood in the Sarajevo cemetery, looking out over the sea of graves, I felt a passionate yearning to call for a worldwide awakening of *ubuntu* — a new form of spirituality, one that was more human, more directly responsive to the suffering caused by social and political circumstances.

But what could this mean — to elevate human freedom to its highest, most creative, and universal expression? A thrill and urgency swept over me. How exciting it would be to radically humanize the Dharma, to make it much more real and accessible to human life — to life here on earth — and not an escape from it. This would require extracting *ordinary wisdom* from its inherited delusions, cultural containers, political manipulations, rampant superstitions, and blinding orthodoxies.

I could see my own indoctrination in religion, Buddhism, and sectarian thinking beginning to crack. And frankly, I wondered what would be left — if we all became universal warriors and transcended the "isms" that formed us. After all, the historical Buddha who supposedly attained enlightenment twenty-six centuries ago wasn't sitting under the tree in India after his attainment saying, "This part of me will teach an aspect of my enlightenment that only the Zen Buddhists will follow, while this other part of me I'll name Dzogchen, and call it the secret teachings and reserve it for the most advanced of my Tibetan followers. And this part will be called *vipassana,* and I'll keep it for the more cerebral of my followers. Then I'll divide the rest of me in such a way that many hundreds of sects will develop, all in my name, that will disagree over the real teachings for millennia to come."

Standing in the cemetery in Sarajevo — a poignant symbol of the sorrowful consequences of propaganda, hatred, and war — I envisioned World Dharma — a metaphor for "freedom through *ubuntu.*" Although I wanted to avoid the traps of dogmatic thinking, I had to give it a name! "World Dharma," I thought. "Here is a vision I can embrace." It's a vision rooted in a deep recognition of our inherent interrelatedness. It empowers relationships as the most sacred place for spiritual awakening, because no one becomes free in a vacuum. As Dr. Martin Luther King Jr. once said, "We are tied in a single garment of destiny. What affects one directly affects everyone indirectly." This had to be the guiding wisdom of World Dharma. This meant that I no longer needed to be confined even by the motifs of spiritual and nonspiritual, Dharma and *adharma,* American or Tibetan, Buddhist or non-Buddhist, or any other arbitrary label that divided life and people up into neat, definable packages. As the Dalai Lama reminded us, "The color of blood was the same for all; human suffering and human freedom transcend all distinctions."

So, too, with World Dharma. It had to develop a new language for the process of liberation that transcended nations, religions, and tribes. In so doing it had to be safeguarded from becoming just another form of indoctrination. With this in mind I decided that World Dharma should not be a new spirituality so much as the means by which to establish an alternative worldview. I thought it could be like the World Music movement, where autonomous musical traditions, each with its own integrity, play together, creating a new sound. World Music gives rise to something greater than the individual musicians who created it. Freedom is without logo. Like the wind, freedom doesn't belong to anyone. Nor can it be grasped or held. If you try to box it you lose it.

After a final prayer at the cemetery, Marina and I took a taxi back to the center of Sarajevo, where our attention shifted from the sacred and serene to a wild and jubilant citywide celebration. As one of the first sunny days of spring after the Dayton Peace Accord had been reached, bringing an end to yet another winter of hell, Sarajevans were among the happiest people I had ever been around. The main city square — where we were sitting — was packed with people dressed in their finest — smoking and drinking and laughing. Rock music blasted from the cafés lining the square. People were partying without fear of being shot by snipers, hit by mortars, or killed or maimed at any moment.

Although almost every building was a bombed-out hulk of twisted metal, broken concrete, and shattered windows, couples embraced and danced romantically in the square. The juxtaposition took your breath away.

Soon after arriving Marina and I got into a lively discussion about English poetry, which she had studied in college. At one point, she shifted the conversation midsentence. Staring at me intensely, she said, "Tell me, after all you've done, what is really worth remembering?" Pausing, she took a long drag on her cigarette while motioning with a finger for me to wait a second before I answered. "I have one request," she continued. "No nonsense! No religion. No Buddhism. No philosophy. No psychology. No dogma. I want to know you — you deep down inside. What makes you get up every day and want to live — to give it your very best?"

She held my gaze for a second, as if trying to read my reaction, then inquired in a polite voice, "I didn't offend you, did I?" Again, before I could answer she playfully quipped, "I hope I did. Maybe I'll get the truth out of you for once." We both laughed. Previously, we had spoken about how rare it was to really have a truthful relationship in life — even between close friends. But as the humor in the moment subsided, her question began to penetrate, amplified by the context — Sarajevo, a population of 350,000, was the size of downtown Boston and was 90 percent ruins. We were at ground zero, sitting in the center of one of the darkest hells of the twentieth century.

As I contemplated an answer, a group of three young men, disabled from the war, rolled into the square in their wheelchairs. Some girls at a nearby table noticed them and ran their way, shouting and throwing kisses at them. Wasting no time, they started dancing together; a couple of the girls actually sat on the guys' laps as they twirled to the music.

Within a few minutes, several other younger kids, each with a leg missing, got up on their crutches and began twirling around like whirling dervishes — keeping beat to a rhythm that was uniquely their own.

My mind crossed all kinds of terrain. It was much easier to stay seated — strapped into a persona of my own perceived inhibition. Or my own struggle. My own shortcomings or inabilities. What was I waiting for — to live fully and without remainder? What more evidence did I need to celebrate each and every breath and not despair about what was missing? Come on, look at these guys, I told myself. Here they are without legs or paralyzed from the waist down. Nothing is stopping them from rejoicing in their freedom. They showed no contrivance. No hesitation. They had nothing to prove.

I remember flashing back to the clinic and the young boy holding his teddy bear. What's he going to do if he heals and comes out of his trance?

The point is to live every moment as if it counts. That's right, the timeless basis of the Dharma itself — to be present, fully. I turned to Marina, ready to deliver my realization with passion and gusto. "When it's all said and done, what is worth remembering?" I said. "Love the one you're with? Do unto others as you would like them to do unto you? Don't play small — take risks? Don't give up, no matter how hard it gets?

"But really, when all is said and done," I continued reflectively, "what matters more than anything? To be yourself! To be human. To dance to your own beat? I don't know — to feel, to laugh, to cry more freely? In the end, I think that's all that matters. What do you think?" I asked.

With a coy smile Marina retorted, "Too much meditation. Too much thinking, as you would say."

Getting up from the table she said, "Come on, let's dance."

I think that afternoon in Sarajevo was one of my first real understandings of *ubuntu,* or liberation through living — a World Dharma beyond words. It was also a glimpse of the difference between wanting to "be human and authentic" and simply living, naturally free.

THE TRANSFORMATION OF CONSCIOUSNESS

The future of freedom is linked to our ability as a species to overcome the forces of ignorance both inside and outside. Despite the fact that we are handicapped by many biological limitations — brains hardwired to prompt irrationality, rage, and violence — we must innovatively challenge our most primitive urges. Genetically passed on to us through our ancestry with apes and reptiles, these urges are useless and obsolete, and we must do all that we can to limit their eruption within our psyches. We must examine, map, and learn the art of overcoming these afflictive forces and hope that in time humans will outgrow these traits, so that they can gradually disappear from the collective gene pool and leave the template of human consciousness altogether.

Deprogramming the mind of irrationality and volatility and reconfiguring it toward wisdom and goodness are ancient ideals. Today such an ambition is no longer confined to spiritual or philosophical circles. The harsh realities of the modern world have shown us how just a few people with hostile fantasies can rain hell down on the multitude. The need to identify the forces giving rise to ethnocentricity, xenophobia, and any other form of human degradation has never been greater. Equally, we must provide concrete and innovative solutions to deal with these denigrating forces, at international, national, and individual levels.

The transformation of human consciousness is a political and social imperative. The promotion of global human rights, exploration of the human mind, and the indivisibility of freedom should be standard subjects taught and discussed in every school serious about the preservation of life. The consequences of neglect are potentially cataclysmic. Near the end of the twentieth century Vaclav Havel, the president of the Czech Republic, in an address to the United States Congress, recognized this: "Without a global revolution in the sphere of human consciousness," he said, "nothing will change for the better.... And the catastrophe toward which this world is headed — ecological, social, and demographic, or the general breakdown of civilization — will be unavoidable."

If we don't examine the real source of human suffering — consciousness itself — there will be no victory over evil. In recognizing this source we will become better able to transcend the politics of recrimination while respecting international rules of justice and law.

Vaclav Havel went on to say, "Consciousness precedes being, and not the other way around... for this reason, the salvation in this human world lies nowhere else than in the human heart, in the human power to reflect, in human modesty, and in human responsibility." Many great minds have recognized that consciousness is the forerunner of thought, speech, and action. Mind is the source from which the world comes into being. It is from the mind that we form identities, create myths, and fabricate illusions. It is from the mind that values are forged, principles are shaped, and freedom is known. As my Dharma guides in Burma would constantly remind us: "To know the mind is the most important task of your life." To know the mind is also to creatively influence one's relationship to the world.

Dostoevsky, the great Russian novelist, directs us to the intimate front lines of the true revolution with his poetic summons,

"Beauty is mysterious as well as terrible, God and the devil are fighting there and the battlefield is the heart. . . ." By realizing that the heart is the source of all that we think, feel, and know, an impassioned sense of self-responsibility arises and with it true empowerment begins.

Entering the epic battle of opposing forces found in the soul of every human being is the greatest of all challenges, spiritual or otherwise. It is both humbling and exhilarating. It inspires awe as well as terror. It leaves one scared and in love at the same time.

In order to explore the heart as the source of true spiritual awakening one must be vigilant in bringing the highest standards of disciplined empirical inquiry to bear upon the process of perception. Nietzsche defined freedom as "the will to be responsible to ourselves." This to me means the ability to respond to the instinct for freedom that is innate within ourselves — ability here meaning competence and skill. In other words, wise discernment and intellectual rigor play vital roles as we open to the contents of consciousness and examine the role of perception as the architecture of reality.

Transforming the afflictive emotions of greed, anger, and ignorance requires courage, intelligence, and kindness. This means not hiding in "axiomatic truths" or "absolute realizations" with their promises of escape into a realm of "perfect beingness." Although I firmly believe in the need to evolve human consciousness to better serve civilization, I do not believe in absolute answers. Developing our reverence for mystery as we explore and map the universe, inside and outside, is the best safeguard against fanaticism and totalitarianism.

I AM THE FREEDOM THAT I SEEK

I want to make clear that freedom *is not* some indestructible realization — the emancipation of consciousness from all forms of self-generated conflict. I am not talking about the absolute end of human suffering or a transcendental experience of unshakeable stillness and joy.

What I mean by natural freedom is just that. We are free when attuned to the rhythm of our own uniqueness — an ease of being that allows us to dance to the music we hear in our own hearts.

Natural freedom arises out of an abiding respect for our imperfect wholeness. Who needs to be perfect when you can be human? So, natural freedom is that condition of being that precedes everything. It precedes *ideas* of liberation; it undermines dogmas, doctrines, mythologies, self-images, attainments, contracts with perfection, and all other inherited forms of self-protection and self-enhancement. Natural freedom precedes these self-delusions, but it also exceeds them. It is a paradoxical and inclusive sense of being. Simply said, natural freedom is the ability to live and die right now with a shameless sense of goodness and beauty.

We must elevate authenticity to the highest status. This process requires a radical acceptance of who we are and feel ourselves to be. From this juncture we express our creative passion — inhabiting every dimension of our being as natural to our whole — the good, the bad, and the ugly.

What else do we have but our humanness, our naturalness, our unique selves? No two of us are alike. No two of us have the same fingerprints. No two minds are the same, no matter how much we have in common. Nor would I assume that any two people love in the same way. The idea seems strange, doesn't it? Imagine a training on the "right way" to kiss? Or the right way to smile? Or the right way to dance? So too with the way we each make love. It is so individual. Dance embodies our most natural freedom and our most authentic beauty. That's why it's sacred. Imagine imposing strict rules on the right way to make love? The religiously correct way to be free?

At one point, as a monk, I began to obsess about getting my meditation posture "perfectly right" — back straight, legs down, head tilted slightly, poised, balanced, with long, slow, deep breaths. The more I tried, the more detailed I became. I often compared myself to the five hundred other monks in the meditation hall. This went on until I had actually perfected it. Now, I said to myself, I can get on with the business of achieving perfect realization. The only problem was that my perfect posture was much more painful than my most natural one. So what did I spend all that time for? It was a form of perfect that didn't shine through to its practical realization. Once I dropped the picture I was able to return to the greater issue, understanding the difference between natural freedom and perfect posturing.

As fragrance is innate to a flower, so too is freedom inherent to the heart. This is as obvious as standing out in the wild and asking, "Where is nature found?" It's all around us, and in us. When we know nature as such, we wake up, begin living again, and in some way we stop dying inside. It is my sense that natural freedom is not something you actually learn, so much as "feel into" and intuit as a progressive set of realizations over an entire lifetime. The authentic spiritual life is not about fitting in or transcending some imaginary self. It's about being a person, challenging fear, and doing something remarkable with our lives.

There is no Mecca outside the Mystery itself. I would rather focus on lived experience. How can one *attain* anything in an unstable and passing world? Is there anything that isn't propped up by conditions? Isn't the universe a house of submolecular cards — an immeasurably complex field of interlocking waves and particles where nothing exists apart from everything else? Is there anything that exists outside or inside of our interrelated infinity? I acknowledge the essential mystery of it all, and go from there. But I don't think of the mystery as "out there." It's internal to myself, too. My brain, for instance, is a mystery. And the idea that the finite brain can actually know the infinite cosmos, with infinite realities is preposterous. No one knows what happens after death anymore than we know where life originates. No one understands how it works.

For the Dharma to have worldly relevance and practical meaning we must foster a love affair with freedom itself. Not a transcendent freedom, but the natural freedom you feel in yourself at this very moment — as you are. To this end I often remind myself: *I am the freedom that I seek. Live outward from there.* As the poet Gary Snyder writes:

> The lessons we learn from the wild become the etiquette of freedom. We can enjoy our humanity with its flashy brains and sexual buzz, its social cravings and stubborn tantrums, and take ourselves as no more and no less than another being in the Big Watershed. We can accept each other all as barefoot equals sleeping on the same ground. We can give up hoping to be eternal and quit fighting dirt. We can chase off mosquitoes and fence out varmints without hating them. No expectations, alert and sufficient, grateful and careful, generous and direct. A calm and clarity attend us in the moment we are wiping the grease off our hands between

tasks and glancing up at the passing clouds. Another joy is finally sitting down to have coffee with a friend. The wild requires that we learn the terrain, nod to all the plants and animals and birds, ford the streams and cross the ridges, and tell a good story when we get back home.

THE STRUGGLE FOR FREEDOM

The struggle to embody freedom is the greatest of all challenges. My Burmese friend U Win Htein — whom I respect enormously and feel deeply indebted to — played a pivotal role in helping me to understand the complexity of "the struggle for freedom," as well as its beauty.

I came to know U Win Htein in 1995. At the time I had been asked by a French publisher to reenter Burma and try to contact Aung San Suu Kyi, the 1991 Nobel Peace laureate. Along with several other key figures leading their nationwide struggle for democracy, she had just been released after six years of incarceration. I invited Aung San Suu Kyi to collaborate on a book of conversations together for the purpose of bringing her message of "nonviolent spiritual revolution" to the world. After an intense and complicated six-week process, I was finally able to meet her, at which point she agreed to the project so long as her two key colleagues — U Tin Oo and U Kyi Maung — were equally included in the book.

Over the course of the next five months I had the good fortune of meeting these three courageous leaders, primarily within the confines of Aung San Suu Kyi's lakeside home in Rangoon. We discussed the concepts of global human rights, totalitarianism, propaganda, nonviolence, Dharma-as-action, social justice, compassion, and the nature of freedom. It was an extraordinary time. My journey came to an abrupt end, however, when the military authorities sent police to my hotel room and forced me to leave the country, blacklisting me from returning. Once back in Paris I retrieved the computer disks containing transcripts of our conversations, which had been smuggled out of the country by means other than myself. With the help of Aung San Suu Kyi's late husband, Dr. Michael Aris, my publisher, Christiane Besse, and my friend Bessiana Kadare, these transcripts became the book *The Voice of Hope.*

During my time in Rangoon I was able to meet many exceptional men and women, each of whom had regularly risked their lives for the right to a free and dignified existence. One such man was Aung San Suu Kyi's senior assistant, U Win Htein, who, like Aung San Suu Kyi, had recently been released from six years of incarceration. Besides being the father of a son and five young daughters, and once a high-ranking officer in the Burmese army, he had also been a Buddhist monk with a long involvement in meditation.

One afternoon — having just completed my conversation with Aung San Suu Kyi — I walked out her door and saw U Win Htein, U Kyi Maung, and U Tin Oo sitting together under the veranda, where they were laughing uproariously. I hurried down the stairs and joined them.

Now, these men are not the least bit ordinary. Among their many virtues they are kings of comedy — master storytellers whose tales take fabulous twists of irony and satire. They, like many others in the struggle for freedom in Burma, use their wit and wisdom as weapons to confront gross injustice. This, of course, stood in stark contrast to the brute military force used by Burma's generals to forcibly rule the country.

Before I could ask the three men why they were laughing, I got swept up in the energy. So, without reflection, I jumped right into the party and the four of us howled and rolled with laughter for the next few minutes. Meanwhile, U Kyi Muang and U Tin Oo began laughing so hard that tears started streaming down their cheeks.

I had to know what was going on. So, I shouted out over their howls, "Come on guys! Why are you laughing? Tell me." But the question did nothing but make them laugh even harder. The only response I got was a finger pointing at U Win Htein. Either they were laughing at him or gesturing for him to answer me. But nothing happened, except that their laughter became so loud it set off Aung San Suu Kyi's guard dogs. They began howling like coyotes.

U Kyi Maung then shouted out to U Win Htein, "Go on . . . tell him — everything!" My sense was that U Kyi Maung wanted to hear U Win Htein tell the tale again as a way to refuel the laughter — to take it even higher. These guys were like that. As the laughter waned and the dogs lowered the tempo of their howling, U Win Htein began to explain. This is what I remember him saying: "When I was arrested back in 1989 the MI — our military intelligence — took me in the night to one of their interrogation centers. They put my hands behind my back and handcuffed me. They put a burlap bag over my head. Then they forced me to kneel down. For the next twenty-seven days they kept me either in that position or lying down, beating me and interrogating me. I was deprived of food, water, and sleep for many days at a time."

My heart sank. "The funny thing about it was the way that their actions reinforced my own convictions," U Win Htein continued. "I mean, the guy was beating me with a baton, kicking me in the hips, forcing me to stay on my knees, all the while shouting over and over, 'Why are you struggling for freedom? Why do you want democracy?'"

U Win Htein paused. The three men burst out laughing

again. They were acting as if this was the most hilarious thing they had ever heard. For me, it was the opposite. I was trembling — primarily, I realized, for fear of it happening to me.

U Win Htein lit a cigar, and continued in a reflective tone, "Now, I would have told him why I was involved in our country's struggle for freedom but I really didn't think he wanted to know why. After all, I was Aung San Suu Kyi's senior assistant. Surely, he had more important questions to ask. For instance, to find out how we're going to send them into retirement."

U Kyi Maung jumped in and said, "Yeah . . . they're not your smartest bunch." His words started the three of them off again — rolling back and forth, and laughing so loudly that it set the dogs off again.

U Win Htein puffed from his cigar and through a plume of smoke and said, "Days passed, I lost count, and they just kept asking me a series of dumb questions, which always included, 'Why are you struggling for freedom? Why do you want democracy?' But after a week or so I began to realize that they *really did* want to know why. My thinking was that since I had been an officer in the same army they worked for, they wanted to understand the motivation that drove me to walk away and join Aung San Suu Kyi and the nonviolent resistance. They couldn't figure out why someone in my position would give up the 'good life' for 'the long walk to freedom.' My interrogator *genuinely* wanted to know the 'why' behind my desire for freedom, because he honestly thought that I had real freedom when I was in the army.

"As I said, this went on for twenty-seven days. Not sleeping, in and out of delirium, and nearing death, so I thought. I held on to life and sanity by grasping with all my heart and strength to the belief in my interrogator's sincerity as well as my desire to honestly answer him. But I would only do it on my terms. I told myself, 'remake the face of this man — from enemy to ally. And answer him only when the hood comes off, not before. I believed in his sincerity, as perverted as it was. I found the strength to keep struggling in seeing 'the purity of his ignorance.' He was, after all, fully indoctrinated in dictatorship. He didn't know any better.

"On the twenty-seventh day he yanked off the hood. Grabbing my hair, he pulled my head back and shouted, 'Why are you struggling for freedom. Why?' I drew on something inside of me I can't explain. But I lifted up my eyes, and said, 'For your sake. Freedom means you too!'"

I held my gaze on U Win Htein. I was stunned. This man endured torture and survived to speak of it because of his belief in freedom, a freedom so generous that it encompassed even the oppressor. I felt both exhilarated and terrified.

U Win Htein concluded humorously, "And he was not the least bit pleased with my answer. I woke up a week later in a small cell with several other prisoners. I had broken ribs, a damaged spleen, problems with my spinal column, migraines, and wrecked knees. I was practically unable to stand for the next few years. And I remained in that cell, without being allowed to leave, for the next twenty-eight months."

I looked at each of these three men, knowing that both U Kyi Maung and U Tin Oo had spent eleven years in solitary confinement. Yet here they were, able to laugh about their struggle. How was it humanly possible? I had been interviewing them for months and not once had they revealed a trace of arrogance or superiority, in spite of the remarkable wisdom each lived and carried. It was almost too much to believe. "That's really what you were laughing about — no joking?" I asked.

The space shifted from ease to seriousness. I thought I had offended them. But soon I learned that I had no such powers. It was just U Kyi Maung's way of setting the stage for the next joke, which was right on me. He burst out laughing and in a playfully sarcastic tone said, "Oh, you Americans are so melodramatic. Perhaps you should meditate more. Be more mindful." This broke them up even more than before. The three of them, all former Buddhist monks, roared with laughter. It set the dogs off again.

And, like we began, the four of us rolled with laughter for the next few minutes until Aung San Suu Kyi popped her head out of the door and said with a gracious smile, "Come on men, there's work to be done — we've got a revolution to lead."

I went back to my hotel room that day both awed and honored by the rare privilege it was to be with such political and spiritual warriors. Among the many valuable lessons I learned from them one stands supreme — no matter how dark it gets there is always freedom if one chooses it. Beauty can be found even in the most terrible circumstances.

◆ DEEP TRUST

The next day I was standing next to U Win Htein just behind the gates to Aung San Suu Kyi's compound. It was the day that Aung San Suu Kyi, U Tin Oo, and U Kyi Maung gave their weekend "talks on freedom" to an audience of several thousand people. Men and women from all walks of life — the young and old, along with representatives of all faiths and religions — would sit on the pavement, through torrential rains and soaring temperatures, risking long prison terms and possibly torture, to join the struggle.

At one point — still churning over the story I had heard the day before — I turned to U Win Htein and asked him, "I don't mean to be rude... but how are you able to laugh at your circumstances the way you do? I mean to say, I'm inspired. But how did you get there? How did you avoid going crazy or becoming depressed, or bitter or angry during all those years in prison?"

He locked eyes with my own. The question seemed to strike a deep memory in him. He pursed his lips slightly and said, "Come." He took my hand and we walked from the gate to the bench under the veranda outside Aung San Suu Kyi's front door. He lit a cigar, and then proceeded to send me reeling again. But this time, it was no laughing matter.

Over the next hour he explained the development of his state of mind over his six years of imprisonment. I'll share the condensed version — paraphrased from what I remember him telling me.

"How did I avoid depression you ask? I didn't. To the contrary, it was the darkest, most difficult period of my life. It was also the time I learned my greatest spiritual lessons."

He went on to explain the process. He was placed in solitary confinement. He had no running water. He received a thirty-second bath once a week. He answered the call of nature in a bucket that was cleaned once a day.

Food consisted of thin warm soup with roots, a bit of rice, and a lot of dirt. Talking wasn't allowed. Essential items were not permitted, items such as flashlights, medicines, pillows, blankets, mosquito nets, pens, paper, and books. No visitors were allowed. U Win Htein continued, "I wasn't allowed out of the cell for the first twenty-eight months."

He explained how for the first two years he fell into darkness — consumed by anger, hurt, and suffering. He hurt so badly, he said, that he was "eaten by the outrage."

Although U Win Htein was a seasoned meditator, he said that "being more mindful of my anger was not where I found meaning. To the contrary, my anger felt right and justified. I think I survived on it. It wasn't that I was proud of the anger but it wasn't that I invalidated it either. The anger rested in integrity. I never lost that. But it is fair to say that for the first two years I lived night and day fuming at my captors."

He went on to explain that during the next two years he descended from anger into the darkest depression he could have imagined. "I lost my will to keep up the struggle. I lost my sense of purpose," he said. "I felt broken. I hurt so badly I thought I would never pull out of it. And just when I thought it couldn't get darker, it did. I became a despondent shell of a human. But somewhere I started to remember the greater cause — our struggle for freedom. It was at this point that I began to feel a sense of dignity. As my anger had rested in integrity — my depression rested in my self-worth. It was a tiny source of light in utter darkness. I survived this period, I think, by trusting in human dignity as the basis of freedom. I also saw that no one other than myself could take dignity from me. I reminded myself, 'do not throw away your dignity. Although you are suffering right now, take refuge in dignity, draw strength from it.'" In this way he explained how he got through his second two-year period.

"Gradually over the final two years I began to feel my heart," U Win Htein continued. "I felt warmth returning. Kindness emerged. I even began to feel compassion toward my jailers. They, too, were suffering. They didn't know any better. They were indoctrinated in dictatorship.

"I survived the final two years in prison by nurturing these Dharma reflections and the feelings that came with them. I think it was the compassion I felt for my people, for my fellow political prisoners, for their families, for Daw Aung San Suu Kyi, for my children and wife, even for the generals — they, too, were suffering behind their pressed uniforms; they lived in fear."

"Anger, depression, and compassion — these were the three phases that defined my years in prison," he concluded. "From this I learned how the Dharma — the way of freedom — runs much deeper than our fear of losing it." He finished with a smile, "This has taught me how to trust — deeply trust."

◆ FREEDOM HAS NO LOGO

It is my belief that only through becoming more human do we have a chance of preserving the miracle of life. We become human by occupying greater dimensions of our entire selves; our bodies, our sweat, our hearts, our hurts, our joys, our creativity, our intelligence, and our imagination — as much of ourselves as we have the courage to embrace.

We must not be so afraid of life and ourselves that we seek escape from them. This means summoning the heart to engage the nuances and profundities of our being — our strengths and weaknesses, the dark and the light, the contradictions and confusions. Why marginalize anything inside of us? Sure, there are some very ugly things in this world. But why allow this certainty to discredit magic or mystery? Why not insist on going forward with heart and soul? This is the archetypal adventure: on the one hand, to seek our own individual happiness, and on the other, to listen to the cries of ourselves and others and do what we can to lend a helping hand.

Freedom must be separated from the packaging and additives our consumer culture has manufactured around it. We must come to understand that freedom is essential to our spiritual welfare. It might be manipulated by ideology, but we must learn to discern false leads and turn away from them. Here, freedom has no logo, no identity, and no nationality. The Dharma is not American anymore than it is Tibetan or Thai or German. The liberation of the

Dharma is unbounded by time and concepts and formulas. Freedom is its own reward. When in doubt, remember — *You are the freedom that you seek.* This demands that we embrace life as an adventure, not as a campaign to remove the anguish from our lives, or to "get it right."

When I lived in Burma, Croatia, and Bosnia during their conflicts, I witnessed the determination of friends and acquaintances who lived day and night ready for anything — to die, cry, fight, love, give, or kill. It was never easy to see them — people like you and me: artists, writers, homemakers, students, doctors, shopkeepers, mothers, fathers, nuns, monks, the old and the young alike — standing up and being called to fight in order to defend their homeland, their family, themselves, freedom itself, from the onslaught of genocide. It was crazy-making to watch but there was something brilliant about it, too.

During my time in Zagreb, my friend Petra had her bedroom blown off her home from a rocket attack. She had just left the house minutes before. She later said that it made her life much easier now that all her stuff was gone. "I no longer have to spend an hour figuring out what to wear," she quipped. "All I've got is what I've got on." Petra wasn't joking. She had a natural depth of caring and wisdom that was beyond what most people could ever hope to develop by meditating. She was certainly much less identified with material things than I was — as were most of the people I knew at that time.

In addition, I always knew it was *them* going off to defend their homeland and not me. I was American, not Croatian, not Bosnian. But faced with the need, could I do it? What would it take for me to fight for my homeland, to activate my Dharma to include participating in a just fight? "You just never really know how someone will behave under fire... until they're under fire," Aung San Suu Kyi once said to me. "But generally, if they say it won't be a problem, or that they won't be scared, they're almost sure to be among the first to run." You just don't know.

Sayadaw U Pandita, my main teacher in Burma, was fond of a phrase that became embedded in my mind: "Those who know, know both those who know and those who don't know. Those who don't know, know neither. The main thing, however, is to know what you know, and how you came to know it, as well as know what you don't know, and how you could know it." The essence of his statement: learn to discern the difference between the direct personal experience of something, and the projections, opinions, and fantasies that it inspires.

We must remain open and inquisitive, but ultimately we must acknowledge the essential mystery of it all. We are clueless at answering the big questions. Who knows what life is, and how we got here? Are we alone in the universe? How did life first start? What's on the other side of death? Is eternal life possible? How much of what we perceive is brain-generated illusion and how much of it actually exists separate from our minds? What is the "really real," the "wholly other"? We have just begun to probe the galaxies. We are mere infants in a universe governed by a cosmological clock tuned to infinity. Our wonderful scientific discoveries are constantly improving descriptions, but they are not explanations.

Clearly, as humans, we live in a world not of our making. We are forced, if you will, by biological nature to participate in our own existence. By necessity we are compelled to eat, drink, and interrelate — but the intensity and contradiction pressed onto human experience get unimaginably dark. It's nearly impossible to hold our hearts open while imagining the daily existence of a child prostitute, or a kid strung out on crack or heroin, wasting away on some city street. Or what it must be like to be one of the hundreds of wrongly accused awaiting execution on

America's death rows. Or to feel the anguish of one of the two million girls subjected to genital mutilation each year. It's no wonder that so many people find it more difficult to embrace life here on earth and engage their humanness than to seek a better life beyond this world and follow spiritual paths that espouse escapes from this hell. A compassionate response to suffering understands our human drive toward escape.

But to resist the desire to escape, to embrace the many dimensions of our humanness and our reality, requires the courage to feel many unpleasant things. We must live with the anxiety of an unpredictable world, where the unthinkable often happens. "There are two ways to live your life," Albert Einstein said. "One is as if nothing is a miracle. The other way is as if everything is a miracle." To me this means working with our "innate broken wholeness." From this basic reality, we can kick butt — enjoy, elevate beauty, frolic, make love — be wild, animal, cool, adventurous, boring, funny, whatever.

"It's only the shallow who know themselves," Oscar Wilde once said. I find his witticism — directed to those who had imprisoned him for exposing their homophobia and sexual hypocrisy — not only wise and liberating but spiritually illuminating as well. His words point to the ego's tendency to become bloated on its own self-importance. They also invite us into humility by reflecting on life's mystery and inexhaustible subtleties.

Grandiosity in its most rancid form becomes megalomania. History is filled with examples of those entrapped in delusions of power and perfection. When self-deception metastasizes into monstrous self-obsession, there are no limits to how far the power hungry will go to preserve their own sick self-image. We're reminded of Hitler's infamous dictum inscribed over the entrance to the Buchenwald concentration camp: "My People Are My God." We all know where this blasphemy led.

It's not through exploring our inner depths alone that we relate to others. To open our eyes and witness suffering we must turn outward. This will allow us to address what may be humankind's quintessential existential struggle: to find our self — mortal, fragile, imperfect — inside a world fraught with staggering expressions of anguish. I think this conundrum is the central equation our spirituality must face. What does it mean to empower a spiritual journey within this infinite inner and outer environment?

"The man who comes back through the door will never be quite the same as that man who went out," Aldous Huxley said, explaining this process. "He will be wiser, but less cocksure, happier but less self-satisfied, humbler in acknowledging his ignorance, yet better equipped to understand the relationship of words to things, of systematic reasoning to the unfathomable Mystery which it tries forever vainly to comprehend."

To be sure, the Dharma — our shared struggle for finding liberation through living — is a complex road. It's a journey filled with oddities, paradoxes, and strange encounters. There are no quick fixes. Insights come slowly. We must prepare ourselves for the long haul — the journey of a lifetime.

THE EVERYBODY

"The mystical is not how the world is, but *that* it is," Ludwig Wittgenstein wrote. Life is infinite mystery and we are microcosms of that same eternity. We are the matter of the universe — a cosmos that made us and will take us. We are wonderfully complex, genetically encoded to seek and create life, genetically encoded to disintegrate and die. Although we appear to be different, we are all kin beneath the skin, sharing the same ancestry. Our history is truly ancient. From a molecule of DNA, origin unknown, life emerged on earth and evolved into a single-cell sea creature. Over the next ten billion years we crawled out of the oceans, formed hands and lungs, and walked upright for the first time a mere three hundred thousand years ago.

Only one hundred thousand years ago the earth's population was sixty thousand. Anthropologists tell us that ten thousand or so people from that original tribe migrated north from central Africa into Europe. From there they went across Asia Minor into Asia, then across the Bering Straight and down into the Americas. Apparently, and not the least bit surprisingly, wherever modern Homo sapiens migrated, he and she drove the indigenous peoples into extinction, either by outproducing them or exterminating them through calculated murder.

We are in the opening years of a new millennium. Thousands of generations have brought us to the era of the postmodern human. Today we are a hypercomplex interlocking circuitry of biological contingency that urgently needs to learn how to intelligently inhabit compassionate awareness. That is, if we are to survive. Because, at the moment, our species is on a tragic trajectory of social injustice and just plain stupidity that might well have a terminal end: thirty thousand children will die today of starvation; twenty-three other children will have their leg blown off stepping on a landmine; and one hundred girls will be raped. Ecosystems are being destroyed. Species are becoming extinct. Our pollutants are warming the atmosphere. Irreplaceable rain forests are being logged. All in the belief that it helps to keep the big wheel turning. Why are we acting like those we put on death row?

The preeminent physicist Michio Kaku tells us, "We have come a long way intellectually from the time of Giordano Bruno... who was burned at the stake in 1600 by the church for saying that the sun was nothing but a star.... But as a species we are in our infancy... and just beginning to break free from the imprisonment of gravity...." Terrence McKenna, one of the most original thinkers of our times, states the issue another way: "We need to face the fact that there is a level of hierarchical control being exerted on the human species as a whole and that our destiny is not ours to decide. It is in the hands of a weirdly democratic, amoeboid, hyperintelligent organism that is called Everybody."

As it is, the Everybody that Terrence speaks of appears to be an isolated phenomenon confined to the surface of earth, where we thrive only within a tiny bandwidth of refracted light. The next nearest source of luminosity to our sun is Alpha Centauri, a star twenty-five trillion miles away. After that is Sirius, over forty trillion miles away. These are just two of about a thousand stars that astronomers are currently surveying for radio frequencies in our search for extraterrestrial life. This of course, is a mere fraction of the four hundred billion stars in our Milky Way galaxy, in addition to the hundreds of millions of billions of other galaxies beyond our own, each containing hundreds of millions of billions of stars. Reason would dictate that the conditions for life exist elsewhere, but contacting that life, if it exists, is far outside our current reality. For all practical purposes we are an isolated colony hurtling through eternity at roughly ten thousand kilometers an hour.

Our life here is a precious opportunity. It is not enough to stand in awe of this totality, we must participate in the evolution of the intelligence in which we are embedded; we must steward our ship ourselves. The time for hope is over. We are in an era of actualization. There is knowledge and there is application of that knowledge. I think we all have a good sense of what we must do. The point now is to embody realization and act on behalf of the greater good.

The Dharma of the whole, or liberation of the Everybody, requires a daring challenge to violence, egocentricity, and myopia. We can do anything if we summon the courage, focus our efforts, and work steadfastly toward our vision. By putting our heads and hearts together, and turning up the fire of discovery, *we can* change the world. As Kabir said, "When you search for the Beloved, it is the intensity of all the longing that does all the work. Look at me and you will see a slave to that intensity!"

A REVOLUTION OF THE SPIRIT

What is most urgently needed in the world today? A "revolution of the spirit" born from a conviction that lasting change occurs when we learn how to challenge our own fear, anger, and ignorance. Aung San Suu Kyi and the people of her country introduced me to this style of revolution. In Burma, the nonviolent struggle for freedom against dictatorship is literally called a "revolution of the spirit." It is a revolution rooted in the wisdom of self-responsibility. By facing the truth in oneself — the wisdom of one's own conscience — one is in the best position to act from love and integrity rather than from fear and revenge.

In her famous essay "Freedom from Fear," Aung San Suu Kyi explains what she means by a spiritual revolution:

> A revolution which aims merely at changing official policies and institutions with a view to an improvement in material conditions has little chance of genuine success. Without a revolution of the spirit, the forces which produced the iniquities of the old order would continue to be operative, posing a constant threat to the process of reform and regeneration. It is not enough merely to call for freedom, democracy, and human rights. There has to be a united determination to persevere in the struggle, to make sacrifices in the name of enduring truths, to resist the corrupting influences of desire, ill will, ignorance, and fear. Among the basic freedoms to which men aspire that their lives might be full and uncramped, freedom

> from fear stands out as both a means and end. A people which would build a nation in which strong, democratic institutions are firmly established as a guarantee against state-induced power must first learn to liberate their own minds from apathy and fear.

Meeting Aung San Suu Kyi was one of the most memorable moments of my life. I had many questions. I wanted to learn from the wisdom of her experience. As many call her the world's female Gandhi, one of the first questions I asked her had to do with the essence of nonviolence. I wanted to know what core quality would make her country's revolution successful when pitted against overwhelming military might. "You encourage your people to first 'learn how to liberate their own minds from fear, apathy, and ignorance.' What is the underlying quality that makes liberation a reality?" I asked her.

Without equivocation she answered, "I would say courage. You were outside on the street when I spoke to the people who had gathered. There were Buddhists in the crowd, as well as Hindus, Christians, and Muslims. There were monks and nuns, even children. All of them want the same thing — freedom. They risked long prison terms, even torture, to participate. That takes courage!"

She told me about the nature of courage. She reminded me that each person has to confront his or her fear. It takes courage to lift one's eyes up from their own needs and to see the truth of the world around them — a truth, such as Burma, where there are no human rights.

It takes even more courage not to turn away, to make excuses for noninvolvement, or to be corrupted by fear. It takes courage to feel the truth, to feel one's conscience. Because once you do you must enter your integrity, your dignity, your worth as a human being. You must engage your fundamental purpose for being alive. And if you are to act on behalf of your conscience — you must confront your fear, or confront your apathy, or confront your indifference. You can't just expect to sit idly by and have freedom handed to you. Liberation will not be achieved this way. Our revolution will be successful only when everyone realizes they can do their part.

In this regard, courage is threefold: The courage to see. The courage to feel. And the courage to act. If all three domains are realized our revolution will succeed.

Revolutionary spiritual change needs boldness — the heart to question projection, ignorance, and fear — empowering one's self as sovereign over the spiritual state of one's own mind. Freedom is a choice. Freedom becomes real through choice. For freedom to become a revolutionary source of power we must, as Aung San Suu Kyi counsels, learn to "act despite the fear."

◆ LOVE IS AN ACTION: GO SLOWLY, ONE PERSON AT A TIME

For nearly ten years of my life I was consumed by the crisis in Burma. In 1990, my colleague Leslie Kean and I had formed the Burma Project USA — a nonprofit human rights organization dedicated to raising awareness of Burma's struggle for democracy. To this aim, Leslie and I, along with a host of wonderful volunteers, produced hundreds of lectures, media presentations, and articles, including the book *Burma: The Next Killing Fields* and a photographic book entitled *Burma's Revolution of the Spirit.* This latter project included essays by eight Nobel Peace laureates and entailed sorting through thousands of graphic images of violence and oppression. The photos, many of which I had taken while in Burma, were a provocative reminder of the ongoing suffering in that mystical land. Around this time the British director John Boorman was making *Beyond Rangoon,* his feature film on Burma's crisis, in which he invited me to participate as an adviser and script revisionist. Not long after, I reentered Burma to meet with Aung San Suu Kyi and her key colleagues in the struggle.

Like a lot of activists, the closer I came to the crisis in Burma, the more I both personalized it and projected it beyond one country's crisis alone. The struggle in Burma became the archetypal revolution that every nation and every person encounters every day — the battle of right and wrong, of love and fear, in one's own heart.

As the psychological membrane between me — the American spiritual activist — and them — the oppressed people of Burma — separated, it was as if I was feeling my own family being tortured and killed. My heart was being crushed, again and again. Many times it was unclear whether to bless or curse the fate that had first drawn me to that distant land. The crisis in Burma compelled me to merge the Dharma with the world of politics, international relations, nature, and global human rights. As Aung San Suu Kyi once said to me, "Spirituality and politics cannot be separated, ultimately. Both deal with the everyday life of people. And at the core of life — at the core of spirituality and politics — are the same qualities, that of human freedom and human dignity."

I credit Aung San Suu Kyi and her colleagues in Burma with opening me up to the wisdom of a whole worldview. Not only did they emphasize how every aspect of existence was interrelated with every other, they continually stressed the importance of everyday action — daily deeds directed toward the greater good. In one conversation she stressed to me that "love is an action, not just a mind state. It is not enough to just sit there and send *metta* — thoughts of loving-kindness. One must get up and do something. *Put that love into action.* Everyone can do it. Everyone can do their bit."

"As spiritual and political beings we are all activists at heart," she went on to say. "No one is outside of society. Not even the monks and nuns in our country. Our revolution includes them. It is about *our* freedom. That means everybody. We must see that nothing and no one is separate from this freedom. No one is an island in this world."

Accepting the pure emotion of being a human without protective personas covering your heart — embracing *our* shared struggle for freedom, rather *my own struggle alone* — is often heartbreaking. Of course, there are moments of joy and celebration, but opening ourselves to feel the whole, or even several more square blocks beyond one's own backyard, is often overwhelming. The torment we see in the faces on the television news every day is staggering. The anguish is almost too much to bear. But there it is, always before our eyes and in our hearts, and if our Dharma is to encompass the world — to become a World Dharma — we must learn to *feel* otherness as an aspect of self.

In Nobel laureate Elie Wiesel's autobiography *Night,* he describes how, when taken as a young child to Auschwitz, he witnessed children being thrown into the cremation ovens alive. He explains how he rubbed his eyes in horror, attempting to wake up, thinking that what he was seeing wasn't real. I read recently that he still, seventy some years later, rubs his eyes as he did in Auschwitz when he sees the world's atrocities. He can't believe the horror he's witnessing could actually be real. And we can be sure that his eyes have seen a lot of inhumanity. The moment our Dharma goes beyond our own self-interest and begins to care about others and the world as an extension of ourselves, inevitably the heart will be forced to open, expand, and assimilate new dimensions. It's one thing to discover oneself through oneself and perhaps several others; it's another thing altogether to empower self-realization through *ubuntu* — the inseparability of liberation. The Dharma of mutual caring is a path of heartbreak and high stakes. It means that we are willing to forgo personal comfort for the sake of opening our souls to the cries and sorrows of the world.

Of course, it's easy to talk about "embracing the world as an extension of self" but to lift off the veil of separation, even a little bit, and to actually *feel* others as self is an act of enormous courage. Earlier I spoke of the Tibetan Buddhist monk known as the Weeper, who was a great inspiration to the Dalai Lama because, through his highly developed compassion, he felt life as an extension of himself and often cried. He knew that every aspect of existence is related. He knew that everything that lives dies. He knew that at any moment something can happen to radically interrupt our lives. It does, and it will.

Now, imagine if we asked ourselves to love one hundred people in our lives as intensely and intimately as we would our own child. If it were even possible to command our minds and hearts at will to open that widely, would we last a month, a week, an hour? I would think that such a depth of caring would overwhelm us. It would me. Being a real person that feels others as self is infinitely more complex and difficult than being entranced by self-centeredness and projection. To be spiritually engaged with life, beyond the privilege and security afforded by our affluence, requires a broad range of emotional muscles, intuitive energies, and discernment skills. The idealism of compassionately embracing the world must be tempered with the wisdom to go slowly — one person at a time.

◆ SUFFERING AND GRACE

Expanding our Dharma life to include an ever-widening circle of people and issues presents enormous challenges. One of the greatest ones I've encountered is depression. It's normal for everyone to have their highs and lows in life — their good days and bad days. But when the lows keep getting lower and longer and the gaps between the highs get wider and their duration shorter, we might encounter depression: prolonged feelings of gloom, melancholy, anxiety, inadequacy, or dread — a whole repertoire of miserable emotions.

I believe that depression is the unavoidable consequence of feeling deeply. The world is often a scary place. It can be utterly overwhelming to open our hearts and feel what's going on in and around us. So it is incredibly important to realize that depression is not only good news along the journey of awakening, it may well be a necessity. This has certainly been true for everyone I know and respect.

I am increasingly convinced that what is usually diagnosed as depression, however, is really the awakening of existential authenticity. It should never be treated as a psychological flaw or character problem to be corrected. If properly understood and worked with, depression, with its intense feelings of hopelessness and despair, can become the genesis for greatness and the doorway into the treasures of a creative, uncompromised life. The first step with any depression is to immediately hear it as a natural call to embrace one's humanness, the natural beauty of ourselves as we are — hurting, crying, feeling defeated.

Depression often feeds on itself, sucking you downward until you are alone in the dark recesses of your soul. Or in your bed. Or in a prison cell. As overwhelming as pain can get, however, the basis of the Dharma life is choice. When choice becomes appealing again, Dharma magic becomes possible, and true change begins.

Depression began to lose its debilitating grip on me when I *chose* to stop judging myself for feeling so much pain, and demanding that I should be stronger and less tormented — and better and deeper. But elevating from shame to grace is a big step. I stabilized by telling myself that it was fine that I didn't fit in and feel connected. I simply affirmed my perceptions and stopped negating them. I told myself I had every right to hurt and cry and be anguished — because it's scary to open one's eyes and heart and see the world in its raw beauty and madness. Whatever the source of our anguish, okay, so be it! Self-honor is freedom itself.

In my own depression I would judge myself constantly, even for feeling miserable. "Hey, come on man, snap out of it," I would tell myself. "You're not a Holocaust survivor. You're not a torture victim. You've got all your limbs and your faculties are functioning." I would compare the ordinariness of my depression to more dramatic varieties, like Hemingway killing himself with a shotgun, or Primo Levi, the Holocaust survivor, whose depression also resulted in suicide. But comparison is not the issue. That's one of the most important attitudes I found in working with depression: It's real and no one is grading the severity or authenticity of our pain. Suffering is suffering. It hurts. It oppresses the mind. It distorts. It can even break you. And once down, it's hard to know up anymore.

In 1990, when I returned to the United States after witnessing the massacres in Burma, this kind of depression overwhelmed me. The really odd thing about it was how elated I felt a lot of the time. I know this sounds like a contradiction, but not so. Besides feeling hurt and tormented most of the time, those emotions oscillated with extreme manic excitement, even rapture at times. It wasn't until much later that I realized that I was manifesting many aspects of post-traumatic stress disorder — from the horrors of war, the death of friends, and the torture of Burma, my spiritual home.

Doing battle with the ignorance and suffering is a complex and largely mysterious affair. My friend Marcia Jacobs is a skilled psychotherapist whose expertise is in working with trauma and sexual violence against women. Reflecting on her many years of working in the Balkans with victims of war, she admitted that there was no single method, technique, or process to help someone liberate him- or herself from pain. The most effective way, she said, was "simply being there — sitting in silence, often crying together."

"Eventually, if and when the tears subsided," she concluded, "I would encourage the women to see the 'healing magic of contribution' — helping each other restore their sense of dignity, worth, and confidence, by 'giving back and to each other' in whatever way they felt was right. These heroic women didn't settle for bitterness alone. In this way, most of the women not only healed, but became even stronger and wiser than ever before."

Suffering is a personal affair. We must see it as human and natural rather than as a flaw in one's character. We need to strike a balance with our suffering that on the one hand respects our vulnerability and on the other fosters courage to enter the fire and learn and grow from the struggle. The Dharma requires that we stop demonizing hardship and misfortune, and in fact eventually develop the capacity to draw strength from them. We learn many of life's most valuable lessons through hardship rather than ease. This means entering the struggle alone, if need be. Aung San Suu Kyi once said, "During my years of house arrest I learnt my most precious lesson from a poem by Rabindranath Tagore. . . ."

If they answer not your call, walk alone:
If they are afraid and cower mutely facing
the wall, O Thou of evil luck, open the mind
and speak out alone. If they turn away and
desert you when crossing the wilderness, O
Thou of evil luck, trample the thorns under
the tread, and along the blood-lined track
travel alone. If they do not hold up the light
when the night is troubled with storm, O Thou
of evil luck, with the thunder-flame of pain
ignite thine own heart, and let it burn alone.

"There are no words of comfort in the poem," she continued. "No assurances of joy and peace at the end of the harsh journey. There is no pretense that it is anything but evil luck to receive no answer to your call, to be deserted in the middle of the wilderness, to have no one who would hold up a light to aid you through a stormy night. It is not a poem that offers heart's ease, but it teaches you that a citadel of endurance can be built on a foundation of anguish. How can anybody who has learnt to ignite his heart with the thunder-flame of his own pain ever know defeat? Victory is ensured to those who are capable of learning the hardest lessons that life has to offer."

We must find the heart to enter struggle with soul enough to forgive. We have epic examples from which to draw strength. The miracle of turning away from retribution that happened in South Africa is one such example. For three years the Truth Council, headed by the Reverend Archbishop Desmond Tutu, encouraged testimony of bombings, maimings, murders, and other atrocities committed during decades of apartheid. He told the people that forgiveness was the only thing capable of ending the bloodshed and making a new beginning.

In his book *No Future without Forgiveness* he writes,

> As I listened in the Truth Council to the stories of perpetrators of human rights violations, I realized how each of us has this capacity for the most awful evil — every one of us. None of us could predict that if we had been subjected to the same influences, the same conditioning, we would not have turned out like these perpetrators. This is not to condone or excuse what they did. It is to be filled more and more with the compassion of God, looking on and weeping that one of His beloved had come to such a sad pass. We have to say to ourselves with deep feeling, not with cheap pietism, "There but for the grace of God go I."
>
> And, mercifully and wonderfully, as I listened to the stories of victims I marveled at their magnanimity, that after so much suffering, instead of lusting for revenge, they had this extraordinary willingness to forgive. Then I thanked God that all of us, even I, had this remarkable capacity for goodness, for generosity, for magnanimity.

THE PIONEERS OF CONSCIOUSNESS

We are in a miracle. And if we are to progress as a species we need to reinspire the urge for open-ended adventure. We need to explore the nature of consciousness and develop a more liberated relationship with as many dimensions of reality as possible, while remaining respectful of our humanness, both in the world, and further out as we explore the cosmos.

"Favor the question, always question, " Elie Wiesel said. "Do not accept answers as definitive. Answers change. Questions don't. Always question those who are certain of what they are saying. Always favor the person who is tolerant enough to understand that there are no absolute answers, but there are absolute questions." Such is the challenge of embracing the Dharma today.

This is how we become pioneers of consciousness, spiritual mavericks. Such people challenge consensus reality and often go against conventional standards of what is thought to comprise happiness. As rebels who are not concerned with fitting in, they are watchful to see if they have been seduced by a preoccupation for power, fame, and distraction. A pioneer treasures personal sovereignty and supports others in accessing their own. They seek the treasures of the heart without neglecting their basic human needs. They challenge dogma and blind conformity.

Pioneers also question their investment in spiritual practices to determine if they are working. Clearly, it takes courage to confront self-deception and investigate pleasant or culturally sanctioned experiences. It takes courage to recognize when one is in devoted collusion with a spiritual tradition or teacher, compromising one's integrity and suppressing feelings of discontent. Mavericks keep a watchful eye on conceit, with its ingenious skill for hoarding power and control. They have the heart to resist the mirage of spiritual grandiosity, courageously lifting the veils of inauthentic certainty. They are willing to stand naked in the fire of the unknown.

Our innate Dharma intelligence is within each of us. This instinct for freedom touches us in the ineffable language of the heart. We sense it as an intuitive pulse — a divine inner perception that arouses us to make the unseen visible, bring clarity to the unknown, and ignite meaning in a world of suffering. The Dharma means accepting the gift of being alive and being willing to transcend life's illusions. It is a mystical calling — rooted in wisdom and supported by compassion — that encourages our highest human ideals and voices our grandest vision for all of humankind, while being firmly rooted in our natural freedom, right now. The Dharma life is a genuine and intelligent exploration of the full spectrum of the human condition. The Dharma is our birthright. It is our quest for existential authenticity.

It is my belief that we are just beginning to understand the structure of consciousness and the nature of the cosmos. We are children in the universe. Let us reignite a dedication to what Joseph Campbell called "the soul's high adventure." This is our time on earth. Let us enter life, not escape it, evolving the highest intelligence possible, both individually and together.

This is our challenge.

PART TWO

CONSCIOUSNESS, MEDITATION, AND THE GREAT UNKNOWN

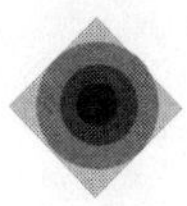

◆ CONSCIOUSNESS IS HOME

Among the great mysteries in the world — the origins of life, space, time, and gravity — the mystery of consciousness is perhaps the least understood. No one knows from where it first came, nor where it goes after we die. The only thing we know with absolute certainty is that this virtual world of complex energies sheathed in flesh exists.

And its exploration has never been more important. As the Dalai Lama said, "Perhaps now that the Western sciences have reached down into the atom and out into the cosmos finally to realize the extreme vulnerability of all life and its value, it is becoming... obvious that the field of what we call 'inner science' — dealing with inner things — is of supreme importance."

The mind is a living organism that chaperons us everywhere, haloing our bodies as the biosphere does the earth. It informs us of everything we think, feel, and say. Consciousness is as central to life as the ecosystem is to the earth. We can't live without it, nor can it be escaped. It is home.

Neglect consciousness — denigrate it, violate it — and like the earth, the individual suffers, and often *causes* suffering, too. On the other hand, nurture consciousness — understand its nature, inhabit it wisely — and we flourish, and elevate society too. Albert Einstein said it this way:

> A human being is part of the whole called by us universe, a part limited in time and space. They experience themselves,

> their thoughts, and feelings as something separated from the rest, a kind of optical delusion of their consciousness. This delusion is a kind of prison for us, restricting us to our personal desires and to affection for a few persons nearest to us. Our task must be to free ourselves from this prison by widening our circle of love and compassion to embrace all living creatures and the whole of nature in its beauty.

But is Einstein's appeal naïve? Is it an impossible ideal? Is it delusional to think that each of us can play a vital role in the future of freedom and the survival of life? Maybe we're simply discouraged, thinking that our lives are too small to make any real difference. It's certainly easy to become cynical, snared into a fatalistic belief that control is in the hands of the politically and economically powerful. Perhaps our hopelessness goes even deeper. Maybe we think that the damage has already been done, and now there must be a massive human die off before the earth can sufficiently regenerate, and sustain a much smaller, more conscientious population. Is it possible to secure our world, even if we wanted to?

These are extreme times. On the opening page of the *State of the World 2002 Report,* we are told that "The human family has suffered sickness, but rare is the plague that can kill a third of a nation's adults — as AIDS may well do in Botswana over the next decade.... Our planet has regularly seen species die-offs, but only five times in 4 billion years has it experienced anything like today's mass extinction.... Nations have long grappled with inequality. But how often have the assets of just three individuals matched the combined national economies of the poorest forty-eight countries, as happened in 1997?" Is there hope?

One of the most precious attributes of the Dharma — finding liberation through living — is that it fosters magic, making impossible dreams come true. Empowering human liberation through the awakening of consciousness is saying that from within our hearts and souls, from the very depth of our beings, there is a primal intelligence that holds the answers to the cosmos and our flourishing as a species. I believe the exploration, understanding, and mapping of human consciousness is the answer to our survival.

Consciousness is our common heritage. It is our bond with all life. It can be friend or foe. It can give life or take it. It can serve or enslave. It can give hope or drown in despair. It can dream or denigrate. It can create beauty or concoct evil. All that we think and imagine originates from within the mind. It's all right there, behind our eyes.

As Gandhi said, "As human beings, our greatness lies not so much in being able to remake the world... as in being able to remake ourselves." He insists that we must "become the change we want to see in the world."

I think we all know, deep inside, that love doesn't begin or end upon the lips of a lover, any more than a war begins or ends on a battlefield. True love and lasting peace must come from a radical change of heart — of the mind, your mind, my mind, our minds together — us, right now. As Aung San Suu Kyi said, "a revolution of the spirit begins... by first learning how to liberate our own minds from fear, apathy, and ignorance." I hear so much hope in her vision. It is a call to become a lover of beauty and change, each of us playing our part in further igniting a worldwide revolution of consciousness, one that honors and celebrates our inherent mutuality, and our inseparable freedom and dignity.

The Vietnamese Buddhist monk Thich Nhat Hanh, in a letter written in 1965 to Dr. Martin Luther King, immortalized the essence of compassionate activism with these words:

> I believe with all my heart that the monks who burned themselves did not aim at the death of the oppressors but only at a

change in their policy. Their enemies are not man, but are the intolerance, fanaticism, dictatorship, cupidity, hatred, and discrimination which lie within the heart of man. I also believe with all my being that the struggle for equality and freedom you led in Birmingham, Alabama, is not really aimed at the whites but only at intolerance, hatred, and discrimination. These are the real enemies of man, not man himself. In our unfortunate fatherland of Vietnam we are trying to plead desperately; do not kill man, even in man's name. Please remove the real enemies of man which are present everywhere, in our very hearts and minds.

DHARMA INTELLIGENCE — THE WAY OF LIBERATION

Embracing the Dharma is a twofold awakening: on the one hand, we see ourselves as a separate being seeking to develop our own individual life, while on the other hand we are trying to understand and participate in a much greater whole. It is both an inner and an outer dance. At times more focus falls on one than the other. At other times they are inseparable.

How each of us goes about seeking liberation — challenging our own weaknesses, evoking our own sense of goodness and beauty — is personal. While there is no singular, true way, I do feel there is one question that leads to many expressions of the same answer — liberation. That one question may best be expressed in the simple words of The Serenity Prayer: "God, grant me the serenity to accept the things I cannot change, the courage to change the things I can, and the wisdom to know the difference." To *know* is the operative word.

In my own Dharma journey I wanted to learn this difference. The quest for self-transformation — the liberation from fear and confusion — is a large part of what led me to embark on it.

When I entered the meditation center in Burma, one of the first things I was taught is that there are two ways to find liberation. The first, and the most difficult, was liberation through world relationships. The classical Buddhist texts refer to this approach as "the way of the Bodhisattva." In contemporary, transreligious terms this essentially means that by engaging in relationships we discover ourselves. Its more elevated meaning: by serving the freedom of others one frees oneself. This style, which is the cornerstone of the "liberation through living" model of spiritual awakening, rests upon the idea that Dharma intelligence — the liberating blend of intuitive discernment, creative compassion, and basic goodness — counters the habit of self-centered fixation. And self-centered fixation is the root cause of greed, fear, anger, and all other forms of suffering.

"Liberation through living" can be likened to the dedication of good parents who are willing to endure anything to safeguard their children. Caring is foremost in their minds. In time their sense of family — a sphere of love and compassion — can expand beyond their own blood to embrace a larger and more complex circle of life. One begins to feel empathy — a deep heart bond — for life and for otherness, not just one's own children or circle of friends.

Such a person thrives on engaging relatedness; all types of relationships become their vehicle for awakening. Of course, the existential, psychological, and emotional physics of interpersonal relationships are complex and difficult, as we know. We will encounter numerous challenges and obstacles. When humans risk loving others as the basis of their being, it's only natural their heart will be broken many times. Nonetheless, one must not be intimidated by rejection, hurt, or any other complexity. No one can take or bargain with our dignity. When liberation becomes more important than safety — as I saw so often with those seeking freedom in Burma — the heart grows stronger and less protective. It becomes more available to actually *participate* in intimate situations. When people impose conditions on their freedom, they are not free until those conditions are met. If they become dependent on those conditions, their freedom disappears.

Striking a human and realistic balance is necessary. As such, they continually challenge fear and make "liberation through living" a way of being.

My Burmese guides often spoke about the importance of compassion. "The mind-set of a person dedicated to liberation through world-relationships makes a life out of caring for others," Mahasi Sayadaw said, "but it must be understood that caring for others is not enough." He made it clear that compassion must be guided by Dharma intelligence, which he described as "being able to discern the right course of action from the wrong one." In order to understand the subtleties involved in making skillful Dharma choices — decisions that release limitation and expand freedom — the person seeking liberation through world-relationships, he said, "understands that awareness is the chief quality responsible for human freedom." In other words, to understand how to liberate "shared space," one must become fluent in knowing where one's person begins and ends, what belongs to self and what doesn't. He concluded by saying that "meditation — the application of sustained awareness — was essential in finding liberation through living."

MEDITATION — THE STUDY OF CONSCIOUSNESS

Mahasi Sayadaw called the second way of Dharma awakening "self-oriented liberation." Usually motivated by feeling the futility of seeking stimulation in the outer world, one renounces such pursuits and enters the solitude of a retreat center. By entering formal meditation, they internalize the mind, employing an awareness that dissolves ideas of the past, present, and future. From within that wisdom, pure consciousness becomes illuminated. And through repetition the meditator progressively discerns the self-generated nature of suffering and gradually liberates him- or herself from primordial misconceptions about what it means to be a human being.

As a process, self-awakening is generally believed to be both simple and complex. It is simple in the sense that consciousness and its inherently liberated nature are not manufactured realities; they are "always already" present, as is commonly explained. It is complex in the sense that the mind seems to thrive on complication. It is human nature to want to be doing something, rather than *just being* without thinking, imaging, creating. By recognizing the mind's capacity for denial, self-deception, and distraction, one ideally seeks and works with a trained meditation instructor in navigating the complex landscape of consciousness.

During my first days of instruction, Mahasi Sayadaw talked about the nature of consciousness and the importance of meditation. He explained how the world exists as an expression of consciousness. I took this to mean that consciousness was the "virtual reality" of all existence — the substratum or submolecular basis of the trees, rocks, rainbows, oceans, and galaxies. Everything was consciousness, in varying degrees. I understood him to say that everything was alive, that we are in a living universe — a cognitive totality of infinite beingness. Quoting the Buddha, Mahasi Sayadaw called this totality *samsara.*

In his way he expressed how human consciousness was a prism for this totality, this *samsara* that we see, hear, and sense in and around us. Just as the outer universe is a multilayered infinity, so too is the inner one. This whole-consciousness or *samsara* is a living eternity of discernable realities. He suggested that the mind can be trained to harmonize itself with any of these realities. He made it clear that "if one knows how, one can enter any dimension of consciousness at will. This is as straightforward as turning a dial on a radio. If you learn how to fine-tune consciousness there will be no static — no distraction, no wandering, no dullness."

Meditation, Mahasi Sayadaw said, is the experiential study of consciousness. Through meditation one can understand the mind's nature — its structure, functioning, and characteristics. Consciousness, according to Buddhist and Eastern mysticism, is a holographic-like excitation of cognitive properties, without a center and therefore without one inherent reality. In other words, consciousness is a coreless circuitry of comprehensible functionings. Meditation is the process by which one enters consciousness — sees past surface appearances — and discerns the underlying realities, or the infrastructure of its processes. Meditation is the science of a self-liberating awakening. "Remember," Mahasi Sayadaw told me, "reality rules nature, not one's opinion of it. When you die, you can take nothing with you. The meditator practices dying every moment. They practice nongrasping. Meditation, therefore, is the practice of liberation." But he was quick to add that "the liberated mind is completely free of the *kilesas* — the afflictive emotions of fear, anger, and ignorance." Anything less he said is "partial freedom — momentary nirvana."

He concluded by explaining how most people in Burma who were serious about liberation "practice a combination of both styles" — liberation through intensive awareness meditation and liberation through world-relationships. "One form serves the other and vice versa," he said.

The Buddha's greatest contribution to society was that he revealed the power of meditation — the miracle of awareness as a means to discover the nature of consciousness. Fundamentally, there is nothing to believe in except that which one's self-awareness reveals about the qualities of one's own being. Mahasi Sayadaw, being the ardent Dharma empiricist that he was, was firmly convinced that there was no God to believe in, no cosmic deities to honor, and no gurus to worship. Meditation — the liberating Dharma — was about one thing: direct, nonconceptual, personal experience of reality, as it is, in this moment, now.

Meditation is the practice of directly participating in the experience of freedom: a way of overcoming energies that function to contract, densify, and burden consciousness while evolving other energies that function to enhance its plasticity, luminosity, and transparency. Based on this basic Dharma understanding, I pursued the path of intensive awareness meditation for the first twenty years of my spiritual life. It was to be a process that touched, opened, and liberated me in every way imaginable. It was equally a process that shattered my ideas of normalcy and turned my life upside down and inside out. The path of intensive meditation is by far one of the most fascinating and complex behaviors known to humankind.

Here's how it happened for me.

THE ESSENCE OF MEDITATION

What follows is a distillation of some of the most intensive meditation experiences I had during my years in Burma from the late 1970s to the mid-1980s. Much of this section is based on hundreds of pages of detailed notes and journals I kept from that period. Although I practiced a number of different methods of insight meditation, for the sake of clarity, I have amalgamated my experiences so as to illuminate the essence of meditation — awareness as the basis of freedom.

As preface to this section I provide a brief critique about what intensive awareness meditation does and does not do — of course, based on my own experience. The main purpose of classical insight meditation is to eliminate the source of conflict within human consciousness, namely mental grasping or clinging, which in turn removes the three root afflictive emotions: desire, aversion, and ignorance. Buddhists believe that 100 percent of one's suffering is self-generated. Therefore, remove the conditions for one's primordial confusion and suffering ceases.

Traditional Buddhism, as well as many other forms of Eastern-oriented spirituality, has it that existence, *samsara,* is intrinsically flawed for two reasons: first, because it is incessantly *changing* and secondly, because it is *empty* of a permanent point of self-reference. As the theory goes, because of one's deluded perceptions of permanence and one's subsequent identification with things, both internal and external, as belonging to one's self — *me* — grasping, grief, fear, anxiety, jealousy, bitterness, anger, and sorrow will inevitably arise when those things change or disappear.

Meditative theory identifies three types of materialism: material materialism, emotional materialism, and existential materialism. Attachment in any degree to any form of materialism results in afflictive emotions, which cause suffering. Therefore the purpose of meditation is to dissolve the ignorant belief in a separate unchanging self. Attachment and personal suffering will then naturally cease.

Beyond the basic instructions of "self-observation," insight meditation begins by bringing you intimately close to yourself, so to speak. Within a relatively short time after entering a meditation retreat, your awareness inevitably alights on that which you resist the most, what you are most unwilling to examine in yourself. Here the meditative friction begins. If you uncover obsessive thoughts and strong emotions around childhood traumas, money, your life purpose, creativity, or relationships, that's what you confront. In other words, through the practice of sustained self-awareness you approach your most predominant inner veil. What happens there depends on the skill of the teacher, the style of teaching, and the courage, awareness, and finesse of the meditator. If the emotional pattern or psychological theme is deeply rooted, it's likely the meditator will stay there, repeatedly rubbing up against his or her "Dharma knot."

Since the practice calls for doing everything within your power to simply observe these thoughts and emotions, no matter how continual or compelling the drama, and since you are not encouraged to investigate the content of the story, you often remain psychologically in the dark about why you experience what you do. Buddhist philosophy ties psychological issues to an idea of self, an illusion, and therefore the ultimate source of the conflict. Western psychology seems to work with rearranging the furniture in your mental house and adopting a more accepting relationship with self. Meditative theory, by contrast, encourages distaste for this existential, emotional, and material furniture. The goal of classical insight meditation is the absolute transcendence of the illusion of self — unconditional freedom — and not the conditional adaptation of self by making things better for the illusion.

One sizable problem with this is that if you choose to return to the world, you inevitably return to your self. And as we all know, in the world, life is as real as real can be. This is where most of us live our lives — in the world, where people are not dreams or phantoms or figments of the imagination, as Buddhism and Eastern mysticism would like us to believe. We are people, relating, learning, hurting, loving, crying, and creating.

Not all meditative philosophies are the same, of course. The orthodox church of *vipassana* — the insight meditation embedded in traditional Eastern and Western Buddhism — and that of "undifferentiated awareness meditation," which has no goal and no other purpose than to be dynamically aware — intelligently and compassionately present — are clearly different.

For now, let's focus on our exploration of consciousness through the looking glass of classical awareness meditation as I learned it in Burma. On the one hand meditation is a brilliant vehicle because it can weaken one's identification with fear, anger, and ignorance. On the other hand one must be very watchful in how it is used. I would caution people against thinking that meditation practice, in and of itself, is the solution to the issues we face. It's what you do with your mind in meditation or within active life that makes the difference. I know this sounds simple, but it can be an addiction or a deflection to be a nun, a monk, a member of a spiritual community — or even a meditator or teacher.

You take your mind wherever you go. Neurotic strategies, self-deception, denial, suppression, and negative programming will follow you like a shadow.

Because of these unresolved tensions, it is unsurprising that many monasteries, meditation centers, and spiritual scenes are sometimes like a version of a dysfunctional family. Primordial negative patterns can be so intact that one chooses spiritual refuge in places, teachers, and practices that keep those strategies alive. Teachers, teachings, and spiritual forms can either serve one's liberation or function as elaborate escape mechanisms. There is no guarantee either way. Denial is a powerful energy and defense strategy.

In general, we tend to project a lot more nobility and spiritual depth on monasteries, meditation centers, and teachers than is actually there. As a matter of habit, we tend to project ideas of purity onto the outer, onto others. I don't know that anyone is free of either positive or negative projections, which can cause great disappointment. It did for me. We need to be watchful of how we lose ourselves in another, in a teacher, in a particular practice, or in a spiritual belief. The mind is so slippery. In a heartbeat projection occurs and the charade begins.

Although intensive meditation was a process by which I came to understand many things about myself and the nature of life, it is fair to say that my insights have merged into a few basics. I believe that you can never escape yourself. In fact, I believe that evolving intuitive intelligence, emotional depth, and caring for oneself and others is the Dharma of the future. The Buddhist and Eastern spiritual belief in overcoming the self is simply outmoded. Life as we know it is only seven thousand generations old. The emergence of a cognitive self is in its infancy. We are inhabiting the universe, not seeking to escape it. We need to activate self, see self as a newborn child, and nurture this self into the most creative, expanded sense of self possible, not see it as the source of suffering. Ignorance — not knowing how to love and give back to life — is the source of suffering, not our own personhood.

◆ BEING WITH WHAT IS

Alan Watts once said, "When you get the message you hang up the phone." In May 1979 I got what I think he meant. I closed my accounts in Los Angeles and was ordained as a Buddhist monk in an attempt to escape the forces of fear, grasping, and ignorance. I saw these as the real enemies within consciousness. I had suffered long enough and wanted freedom from within.

Thus, I began my quest for nirvanic weightlessness — what Eastern mystics call the absolute absence of desire, or the liberation from suffering. In so doing, my teachers in the monastery assured me that if I followed their Dharma instructions I would, through my own effort, extricate myself from egocentricity — the root affliction — and come to know, beyond any doubt, the same timeless nirvana the Buddha realized twenty-six centuries before. Their unwavering confidence in "true freedom" was the most reassuring psychology I had ever heard. And I loved that they had no interest in coddling my ego. They supported the quest to obliterate the primordial strategy of a separate self. They thrived on helping me to vanquish limitation. They wanted nothing from me except a sincerity to be all that I could be. There was no other exchange. No money. No applause. No favors. These guys seemed like straight shooters, true pioneers of consciousness. They did what they did as a matter of conscience and compassion, as far as I could see. This touched me like nothing I had ever known. It was a perfect fit. I had finally found a Dharma tribe.

As I began my retreat in Burma, every day felt like I got a bit closer to my heart. It was extremely hard at first, but I never doubted its worth. Intensive meditation soon became the most natural endeavor of my life. I loved the basic message of meditation. Do nothing, go nowhere, listen to one's being, and intuitively examine what you see, feel, and hear.

Krishnamurti offers one of the most beautiful descriptions of the quality of listening that is required in classical meditation: "I do not know if you have ever examined how you listen, it doesn't matter to what, whether to a bird, to the wind . . . to the rushing waters . . . in a dialogue with yourself. . . . If we try to listen we find it extraordinarily difficult, because we are always projecting our opinions and ideas, our prejudices, our backgrounds, our inclinations, our impulses; when they dominate we hardly listen to what is being said. . . . One listens and therefore learns, only in a state of attention, a state of silence, in which the whole background is in abeyance, is quiet; then, it seems to me it is possible to communicate."

Since intensive meditation was a systematic process by which consciousness directly experienced itself prior to intellectual reflection and philosophical speculation, I soon became enchanted with learning the ancient art of transconceptual listening, along with fostering "the wisdom of no escape": How could there be any other place than where you are? I also fell in love with the newfound dignity that came in knowing that I had finally stopped seeking after the future or hankering over the past.

After a few months in the monastery my meditation began to click and the practice of intuitive self-presence took off. Awareness was seen as a radical transformative power that harmonized consciousness, evolving its lucidity, sensitivity, and luminosity.

Awareness also peeled back mental postures and personas, revealing a more tender and natural experience of being.

As understanding evolved, the petty things I had initially judged as counterproductive to meditation — the hammering, barking dogs, oily food, flies, and mosquitoes — were seen as gifts, opportunities to release anger and attachment and experience a more liberated presence, the essence of the Dharma life. Even the previously dreaded daily schedule of twenty hours of meditation became a delightful joy.

Thus, I awoke to the elegance of sustained awareness. The practice of meditation became a wonderful new way of life. I was amazed to see how awareness put eyes and ears where there had been none. It enhanced perception and revealed greater nuance and dimension. Sounds were accentuated. Colors became brighter. Tastes, more subtle and sweeter. Smells more fragrant. At times it felt like every cell in my body was undulating with orgasmic bliss. Watching the fog lift in the early morning was a dance in itself — the play of photons, like tiny prisms refracting thousands of infinitesimal rainbows on the eye. The smell of the gardenia bush just outside my window became a symphony of textured scents. I fell in love with the simplicity of just being. There was no hurry. No place to go. No persona to uphold. No bills to pay. No appointments to keep. No one to please. Nothing to say. Nothing to fear. This was my first real glimpse of the natural mind — a mind free of conceptual involvement, at ease within its own uncontrived nature, abiding in a space of undistracted presence.

Feeling life so immediately and fully brought a natural stature to everything you did. Suddenly everything opened — everything mattered: the way you sipped tea, the way you bathed, the way you relaxed the habit of outcome. The day became more like art than practice. Everything was a brush stroke on the canvas of pure being. Time seemed to stop. Here, I surrendered into the gentle flow of life's moments. It made me smile, in the deepest way, to know that I had finally arrived. Nothing else mattered except *to be* — an awareness of this moment now.

So it went, month after month — another sunrise in Shangrila. My awareness was occupying greater dimensions of being and an intuitive self-honesty would gently realign awareness back on being whenever it wandered. The day became a dance of being present, sensing, feeling, intuiting the flow of conditioned formations arising and passing on the surface of the mind.

I discovered that awareness, and for that matter stillness too, were not static states. Nothing was — everything changed. I discovered that you could *enter* awareness, enter this sense of intelligent stillness. You could actually intuit your way around, interrelate with it, play, learn how to influence its weight, luminosity, and transparency. You could dissolve your sense of self into it, like a wave merging back into the sea, or a rainbow disappearing in the sky. It was almost like sleep, but finer and more tranquil. Or you could *occupy* this presence — fill it out and expand its size. At times you felt infinite, at other times invisible. How easy it would be, I thought, to get lost here, to become bedazzled with the physics of inner space, this singular state of mind.

Mahasi Sayadaw explained to me how attachment, the fixation or fusion with interior processes, functioned like friction in the mind and thus blurred natural consciousness. He likened the mind-set of a meditator to a mirror. First of all, he said, "a mirror reflects reality and not one's opinion of it." A mirror never lies and therefore is free of self-deception. Also, a mirror, like awareness, is by function present. It does not follow an image into the past; nor does it anticipate an image in the future. In other words, a mirror sees, but does not grasp. It knows, but does not keep. In that sense, he concluded, "awareness is the most trustworthy state of mind."

Day by day, as the meditations developed, I became aware that I had no noticeable sense of conflict that needed resolution. By some form of Dharma magic the desire to be free from anything seemed irrelevant. Desiring freedom was a bit like desiring sex, once you are feeling free or having sex, you stop longing for that which you are doing: being replaces seeking.

Here, I found myself entering a subtle cycle of freedom. It's a bit like breathing. One doesn't hurry up and inhale in order to exhale, any more than one hurries through one breath in order to get one breath closer to the end of breathing altogether. Nor does one deliberately breathe in and out in order to develop the perfect breath. I decided that, beyond the metaphysical and cosmological belief systems shrouding Buddhism and insight meditation, it was a practice of radical naturalness. Paradoxically, that naturalness or nonrigidity of being required extreme self-honesty and discipline to realize. I began to really appreciate the power and beauty of challenging the twin mental habits of yearning and avoidance — the antics of fear and contortion.

So, each day became a wonderland of new discoveries. I had never been so enraptured — and so easily — just being with the natural flow of what is. As this effortless presence evolved it reflected greater nuance of being — consciousness and physicality. Breathing became slow and nearly imperceptible. At other times it would disappear altogether. Sometimes it would feel as if I were breathing with every cell of my existence. Then on a dime, the body would disappear — become nonexistent — leaving only this sense of transparent presence. This sense of cognitive fullness nourished me in ways that no externally directed desire had ever accomplished. Pure consciousness was the ultimate drug. If only I had known sooner, I lamented with a smile. And furthermore, if I could do this, I mused, anyone could. I was the most restless person I had ever known. I was the most impatient person among all my friends. I needed the most distraction. I thrived on it. In fact, I loathed sitting still.

Through the meditation I became essentially unrecognizable to myself. It was an "existential rebirth." My present sense of being didn't compute with the past, except through the invisible thread of self-awareness. It was no wonder that the Buddha referred to mindfulness as a miracle, having the transformative power to absolve consciousness of self-imposed limitations. I had no discernable past I was aware of, except for the innate functioning of memory that allowed for basic coherent existence. Nor was there a place to get to in the future. The cosmos opened into what felt like a universal timeless present that I — pure consciousness — was inseparable from.

Although my present way of being stood in stark contrast to the raw edge of my life in urban America, there was something so utterly natural about it that I felt like I'd been there forever. You know how it is sometimes when things fit so nicely that you can't believe that you actually settled for so much less for so long? This was that moment, but without the neon. I was just hanging out within a phenomenological event of interdependent subtleties — ordinary life! — characterized by impermanence and emptiness. Without the process of creating ideas and concepts crisscrossing through consciousness, the mind was a remarkable cognitive vastness, especially when unified through focused attention. There was a growing rhythm inside of a "freely arising awareness" that simply engaged the present and let it be.

THE WEIGHTLESSNESS OF NONGRASPING

It was at this stage of meditation practice that I began to understand what was meant by "Dharma effort." It was twofold. On the one hand it was simply the exertion required to be aware, to rest in presence in any given moment. On the other, it was the effort required to realign awareness with the present moment whenever it drifted either into the past or projected into the future. If this twofold effort is sustained, a meditative momentum builds — awareness and focus mature. The cause-and-effect nature of liberation seems to take care of itself naturally. As the force of freedom gathers energy, the sense of effort fades until awareness begins to arise independently, on its own. At this point the insight arises that there never was someone making an effort to be present in the first place. Effort, awareness, and insight are all seen to be arising radically free of self-reference.

This was a fascinating new discovery, which relieved me of the burden of doubt about the issue of "being versus doing." I saw clearly that it takes effort to *challenge* the habit of nonbeing, and that's called "doing the Dharma." But once the doing is done, being takes over and does the doing. One sees that there isn't someone who is either doing or being or nondoing or nonbeing. The Dharma is doing the Dharma, that's all. So one isn't afraid of assisting the Dharma, so to speak, by making a bit of effort for a while.

Equally, I was aware of how elusive a dance this all was. Although these states of consciousness seemed accessible to anyone who fulfilled the necessary requisites, I had to look no further than my own life to see the complexity of what I had to go through to get this far. How many psychological births and deaths I had to undergo. How many ontological skins I had to shed. The heartaches and heartbreaks. In fact, it was nothing short of a miracle that I was in Burma at all. This reflection emboldened me. I had found my true calling. The words of Herman Hesse rang more loudly than ever: "Each man has only one genuine vocation — to find the way to himself.... His task is to discover his own destiny — and live it out wholly and resolutely within himself. Everything else is only a would-be-existence, an attempt at evasion, a flight back to the ideals of the masses, conformity, and fear of one's own inwardness."

"Be present!" That was the core instruction I received. And so it went. Over the next month the meditation refined. Consciousness became so energized I could barely sleep. At one point, I stayed up for three days consecutively in an unabated state of rapture. My instructor said, "It's normal... be aware of it." After a few more days of practice I became so ecstatic I lost my hunger, and began to skip lunch in order to continue sitting in meditation. Clinging to any aspect of existence — the body, states of mind, awareness itself — was seen as absolute folly. Everything was felt as insubstantial as a dream. Nothing could be kept permanently so it seemed laughable at this stage to think that fixating on anything other than unconditional freedom had any value.

Further, desire of any kind felt like the poorest imaginable substitute for human happiness. Desire was like a rat on a tiny wheel, "the hungry mind" spinning faster and faster in anticipation of getting the object of desire. It's the rush that gets you off. And there's no end to desire. Round and round, more is better, wanting this, not wanting that. First here, then there, in a cycle of hunger that only increases. Like chocolate, the more you eat, the more you want, so my thinking went. But to be in the zero center of inner being — the weightlessness of nongrasping — felt like the greatest peace of all. Although this state of frictionless suchness exceeded any drug experience I had ever had, it didn't exclude many of the same properties. The mind felt like a luminous sea of infinite possibilities — a submolecular dance of waves and subtleties. Wherever I looked I saw the poignant perfection of a magnificent miracle we were all a part of. My heart opened to the brilliant weirdness of it all. How could one not have love and compassion for the suffering, as it were, all of us a family spinning alone in outer space?

I dove in further. I had to know this consciousness at its most primal level. I wanted to know myself, at the very source of this fountain of being. A great stillness came over me. The waves of rapture instantly ceased. The ocean of consciousness calmed. Here, there were no conventional thoughts. Rather, it felt like existence itself was primordial intelligence made manifest. The human was separated from this larger universal reality only by the centrifugal force of its own ego. This kept us spinning like miniature whirlpools, in our own circles of self-interest, while all around us was the greater sea of consciousness. Was I to identify with a transpersonal infinity, or a separate limited I?

One night in meditation I oscillated between indescribable dimensions — sometimes it felt like an oceanic, vibrant imperturbability and other times it felt like a cognitive invisibility that was utterly empty and full at the same time. I asked myself, Was this realization what the Buddha meant by enlightenment — the ultimate truth, the highest refuge? As the realization stabilized I was certain that it had to be perfect realization — the absolute absence of self-fixation and suffering.

When I went back to my room that night I remember sitting

on the edge of the bed and crying with a joy that rectified every aspect of my life. I could see how everything I had ever done had brought me to this point. Somehow life was a perfect strangeness. A flawless accident. Nothing was out of place. It was all grace. My upbringing, my car accident, my shame, my addictions, my headaches, my backaches, my heartbreaks — all sorrows, joys, and pains — were perfect events in the tapestry of infinite mystery. How could they not be? How could life not be exactly what it is? Life was an unfolding miracle, if only we could see it from such a perspective all the time, I thought.

Further, Dharma beauty was life; it was not something outside of it. The Dharma was *always already* present, right here and now both inside and outside our head. Where else could it be? Everywhere, always! That's the only truth. What other realization could there be, I wondered. Everything one could ever dream or hope for was accessible and separated from us, not by land or money or a thing or a teacher or a teaching, but as William James said, "by the filmiest of screens," by consciousness itself. My dream of nirvana had come true, I thought. This had to be the highest realization.

Although I lay down that night, I remained awake until morning. I recall that night, lying awake, filled with exhilaration, anticipating that my teacher was bound to confirm my awakening.

◆ ARE YOU ENLIGHTENED?

The next day, late in the afternoon, I went to the cottage of my meditation teacher, Sayadaw U Pandita, for our scheduled session. As I sat on the floor waiting to report my meditation experience, I had no doubt that he would confirm my enlightenment. U Pandita closed the book he was reading and looked at me saying, "Take your time. There is no need to hurry today. Please give me a full accounting." We both laughed.

As I was about to speak he said, "Wait. I want you to describe your meditation as if you were a traveler returning from a long adventure. Take your time. Tell me about the valleys and mountains you crossed. What did you see along the way? Tell me about the flowers, and the birds and the trees. Describe them. And the animals, too.

"Also, describe where you camped at night. Did you look up at the stars? Did you dream? If so, explain to me what you saw in your mind's eye. Take me along the landscape of your experience, just as you discovered it, as closely as possible. But please, just the facts. No translation. No embellishment. The more detailed you are, the better able I am to guide you."

I was stunned. A wave of gratitude lifted my posture. No one had ever wanted to know that much about my life. He had probably interviewed well over fifty meditators that day, yet his eyes reflected the wonderment of a child, and his heart communicated the seriousness of a Sherpa whose hands guided you across the precarious, icy slope of egoism, denial, and self-deception.

From the moment we first met a few months before we had clicked. He was the first person I had ever encountered who not only greeted my own level of intensity and questioning with his own, but celebrated it.

Under his careful guidance over the previous few months I had learned that he was incredibly intuitive. He read energy. He not only looked at you — your mannerisms, the way you moved your hands, the direction of your eyes when you spoke — but he entered your very being. He had the beautiful desire to truly want to know you. In his presence I felt I not only had found a highly skilled Dharma guide, but a best friend.

And so it came to be. I took my time and shared the most salient features of my meditative experience. By the time I had finished speaking, perhaps thirty minutes later, he had not moved his head, hands, or body even once. He listened without comment or physical expression.

He then asked me in a calm voice, "Do you think you're enlightened?"

I replied, "May I ask you what you think, sir?"

He replied in a calm, gentle tone, "Prior to the Buddha's awakening he practiced intensive meditation under the guidance of one of India's most famous teachers. At a certain stage of his practice, Siddhartha — the Buddha to be — went to his teacher and explained his meditative experience, that his mind had become infinite, transparent, and sublimely still — almost identical to what you told me about your experiences. Siddhartha asked his teacher the same question you asked me: "Is this enlightenment, sir?"

"According to the classical Buddhist texts, Siddhartha's teacher responded by confirming that, indeed, he had reached the highest realization, the most sublime state of human consciousness. His teacher told him he was enlightened. Further, his teacher then appointed Siddhartha to the status of guru, like himself."

I didn't know exactly where my teacher was going with the story but I had a strong sense of the drift. "But Siddhartha was smart," he continued, looking at me with an unflinching gaze. "Siddhartha knew that he was not fully satisfied with his depth of experience. He was discerning. He had Dharma intelligence. Siddhartha politely dismissed his teacher's pronouncement of enlightenment as misguided.

"In so doing, Siddhartha also gave up the opportunity to be a guru — a fully realized master. This took bravery. He knew that his realization was pseudo-nirvana — not real enlightenment. He had his heart set on the complete deliverance from the *kilesas* — all nuances of greed, anger, and delusion. Although his consciousness was luminous, infinite, transparent, and still — and seemingly liberated — beneath the ocean of this state were the currents of fear, desire, and ignorance. In his dialogue with his teacher, Siddhartha had the greater realization that he was not liberated from the very conditions that, if present, cause conflict or other nuances of *dukkha* — suffering.

"Nonetheless, many meditators get stuck in this state of pseudo-enlightenment," Sayadaw U Pandita continued, with a wry smile. "If you don't confirm their state as nirvana, some monks and nuns here in Burma get upset.

"Still further," he went on to say, "a number of these monks and nuns will go out and begin teaching their 'realization' as the enlightened state. Some of them will become very successful. They even end up acquiring large followings. Although I have never been to a Western country, I would assume this is true in Europe and America as well. Some even get angry and turn away from you if questioned. Spiritual pride is a strong force in the mind, don't you think?"

I smiled and quipped, "I don't know, I'm not enlightened."

I had never seen him laugh so loudly. "Are you sure?" he asked.

"Maybe you should go on with the story and I'll let you know at the end," I said.

He continued in a more serious tone. "In addition, we also have other monks and nuns in our country who simply read books that describe these states of consciousness, and, based on mere study alone, learn to give eloquent Dharma talks on attaining these states. There are even cases of how some of these 'book-trained teachers' forget that what they know was gleaned from literature. We call these people soap sellers who don't use their own product. They are also like schoolchildren who become so enamored with the role of a movie star they go about mimicking that actor's screen role in their own life. So one must be very careful about assuming anything about one's own depth or labeling one's state of mind," he concluded.

SPIRITUAL URGENCY

"The reason why Siddhartha rejected his teacher's assessment was that he was seized with the quality of consciousness known as *sanvega,*" U Pandita continued. "*Sanvega* is a Buddhist Pali word that means spiritual urgency. Since the point of the Dharma is to liberate the mind from the *kilesas, sanvega* is a heightened sense of Dharma intelligence that functions to bring the mind as fully as possible into the present. With *sanvega* one is passionate about freedom.

"*Sanvega* opposes complacency and spiritual pride — or the overestimation of one's Dharma understanding. Without *sanvega* it is easy to wander and get lost as one crosses the landscape of one's mind."

"So *sanvega* is like the fire in the mind that burns for freedom?" I asked.

"Yes, that's a good way to say it. The Buddha said that he taught only one thing — suffering and the cessation of suffering. *Sanvega* is rooted in compassion for one's own circumstances — the resolution of one's own suffering. I'll give you an example from the Buddhist texts, found in *Majjhima Nikaya,* or the 'Middle Length Discourses.' This teaching comes from the *Abhayarajakumara Sutta,* or 'The Buddha's Advice to Prince Abhaya.'

"On this one occasion, a prince invited the Buddha to his home for a meal. Apparently the prince wanted to find a flaw in the Buddha's teachings and therefore refute him. The prince asked the Buddha, 'Would you ever speak in such a way that was unwelcome and disagreeable to others?'

"The Buddha responded, 'There is no one-sided answer to your question.'

"Now at the time a young child was lying on the prince's lap. The Buddha asked the prince, 'If, without your knowledge, the child swallowed a stick or pebble, what would you do?'

"The Prince said that he would do anything to remove the obstruction in order to save the child's life, even if it meant placing his finger down the child's throat, or drawing blood if he had to.

"When the Buddha asked him why he would act in such a manner, the prince said, 'I have compassion for the child.'

"Now," U Pandita said, turning to me. "Imagine . . . imagine if that were your child. Imagine that he or she was gagging and possibly dying right there before your eyes. What would you do? How would you respond?"

I thought about it for a second and said, "I'd do anything to save my child's life. Absolutely anything."

"Of course, like the prince, you might stick your finger down the child's throat. You might slap his back. Maybe his throat clears or maybe it doesn't. If it doesn't you keep trying. Right? Time is running out. As you do, perhaps you start yelling. You would probably pound your child's back quite hard. Maybe you knock the wind out of the child's lungs. But the goal is reached, the obstruction comes out, the child's life was saved.

"Now imagine the situation from the child's perspective. The child was too young to know what you were doing. It's possible that your child might even become angry or feel hurt that you slapped him so hard on his back. Nevertheless, his life was saved.

"Now, let me ask you, what motivated you to save your child's life? Was it anger or compassion?"

"Compassion and perhaps a bit of healthy fear," I said.

"Nor did you waste a second in taking the right action, did you?"

"No, of course not."

"This is the state of *sanvega.* By mixing compassion, urgency, immediacy, and purpose together you bring this intensity to the present moment. Just as you did with your child, you bring this *sanvega* — this liberating Dharma intelligence — to yourself, to your own being. As such, your free yourself from your own internal obstructions.

"Look at it another way," U Pandita continued. "The Buddha likened the *kilesas* — fear, anger, and ignorance — to a forest fire that burns everything in its way — life, property, trees, animals, everything. A fire is merciless in its destruction, as we know. If in doubt, ask a fireman how they feel about a fire. Ask people who have lost loved ones to fire.

"The mind is on fire with *kilesas.* One of the Buddha's most impassioned discourses was called the fire sermon. He said the eye is on fire with greed, anger, and ignorance, as is the ear, and the mind. That's why we frequently say 'burning with anger, burning with hatred, burning with lust.'

"Just as a fireman urgently puts out the fire and saves lives, so does the follower of the Dharma vigilantly extinguish the fire of one's own fear, one's own self-centeredness, one's own ignorance. These fires are within your own consciousness. They've caused you and others problems and suffering for a long time. Just look around and see how much destruction comes from these inner fires. It's tragic that more people don't see the real source of their burning. It's the only way for lasting peace."

I nodded my head in silent agreement, flashing back to my own out-of-control projection when I first entered the monastery. Projection came so easily. In a flash we blame. In a flash someone else becomes the source of the problem. I was beginning to appreciate that beneath my sense of transparent stillness there was a lot more of me that had not yet been found. His teaching on *sanvega* was beginning to ignite.

He continued, "Use any metaphor or simile you wish to inspire yourself to evoke *sanvega*, or awaken Dharma urgency. Inspiration is inspiration. It doesn't matter whether the metaphor comes from art, music, science, dance, or athletics. The important thing is to be vigilant in one's awareness of the present moment — the intuitive investigation of consciousness as the source of suffering, and as much as possible remove the conditions for the *kilesa* fires to arise. The absolute absence of fear, desire, and ignorance is the coolness of nirvana."

He looked at me with a deeply compassionate gaze and said, "Please do not settle for anything less than a true taste of freedom. But remember, be patient, neither tense or too relaxed. Exaggerated *sanvega* creates anxiety, and this is an obstacle," he warned me. Then with a smile he said, "It's awareness that liberates, not your desire for freedom. In other words, remove the *you* from the meditation. The Dharma liberates the Dharma, not *your* effort to be free.

"We can be very grateful to Siddhartha for rejecting his glimpse of pseudo-nirvana. It was an act of great compassion. Please try. Be aware of your stillness. Be aware of your sense of peace. Be aware of whatever it is that is present in you, that's all. Everything else will take care of itself," he concluded.

I thanked him for his generous teachings, then bowed, and returned to the meditation hall, vowing to know that state beyond stillness — the unconditioned nirvana.

◆ IS MEDITATION THE PRACTICE OF NARCISSISM?

Despite the many previous weeks of meditative grace and my newfound knowledge of *sanvega,* oddly, over the next few days the meditation began to go flat. It wasn't a bad thing. It was just empty of eventfulness. Weeks went by this way. It was neither pleasant nor unpleasant — just another day in the life of an ordinary monk meditating in a monastery with a few thousand other monks, nuns, and laity. Sayadaw U Pandita was nonchalant about my condition, assuring me that I was experiencing "meditative doldrums."

"Nothing to be concerned about" he said. "It's normal and, like all other conditioned formations, it too will pass. Be present, that's all." He also convinced me that I hadn't fallen into the trap of becoming a "chronic yogi" — a pejorative term used to describe an institutionalized meditator who was hiding in the practice. I heard him tell a number of people that intensive meditation had a specific purpose — to relax self-fixation. Once you've released that fix as much as possible, you go back out into the world and do something special with your life. Meditation wasn't a career. Staying in retreat all the time made as much sense as prolonging open-heart surgery: once cured, you go home and enjoy a healthy life.

But as the weeks wore on I became somewhat irreverent toward the whole process of self-awareness. I wondered, How much of yourself can you take and still think there's something new and exciting about it? Nonetheless, since I'd come such a long way for the opportunity, I carried on with the practice of being present. The monsoon season passed. The cool season arrived. Nine months into the retreat the days became warmer and the hot season began. Still, nothing special happened. The meditations continued to be a quiet, boring study in stillness. Week after week, sitting after sitting, I mindfully observed an ever-empty parade of vapid phenomena silently streaming by.

And U Pandita continued to ask me to report every boring detail of the boring landscape of my boring inner being. I became so fed up with hearing about "being aware of being still" that if it hadn't been a silent meditation center I would have screamed.

After another week I got so fed up with hearing about the virtues of the "moment" that I was ready to pack it in, disrobe, and get a life. To hell with this "being in the now" story, I thought. It's all hype. You don't see any New Agers nominated for the Nobel Peace Prize for being in the now. I should get on with shaping a vision for the future. I should get off this "overcoming of my own personal suffering" kick, get back to the real world, and start making a contribution.

The more I thought about it, the more my own boredom turned into annoyance. Suddenly the entire spiritual endeavor of seeking my own personal salvation seemed strangely sick. It's all about me — me mainlining me. Me overcoming my self-centeredness by focusing on me! *Me* all the time on *me.*

Had I been duped? Was meditation the practice of narcissism? Had my head been hijacked? Face reality, I said to myself. You're spending the best years of your life looking at yourself in the mirror of mindfulness. How much more self-obsessed can it get? At least people in the real world have jobs, make love, make money, have families, and have a house full of goodies to show for it.

Whereas all I have is a shaven head that's ambushed every night by mosquitoes. Never mind having a lover, I'm not even allowed to masturbate. Was I stupid or what?

Snap out of it, dude! This being present business is bullshit — an ancient scam that brokers supernatural escapes to idiots like me. If I hadn't been a monk taken care of by the monastic community and its supporters, I would certainly have split. To pay money to learn how to "be present," I thought, is about as absurd as it gets.

Eventually I decided to confess my frustrations to my teacher. In response, U Pandita requested that I sit through a beginner's course on meditation, where the basics of the practice are explained. There I was, nine or so months into my own retreat, sitting in with a room full of new meditators listening to instructions on the first day of their retreat.

The instructor began by explaining that meditation is based on three words: look, see, and know. If you want to know the nature of consciousness you must look at it. When you look at it you cannot help but to see it. When you see it long enough you will invariably know it. In other words, to know the movie on the screen of consciousness you must observe the characters. You must look at your thoughts, images, emotions, and ideas. These are characters within consciousness. Other characters are judgment, anxiety, calmness, anger, love, jealousy, goodness, and so on.

If you pay attention to the interaction of these inner characters on the screen of your being, you'll come to know each energy, what it is, and how it behaves. And as with any good drama, you'll see many wonderful and startling things. You'll see that if you occupy a character — fuse with it, become fixed within it — you lose the plot, you lose perspective, and you fall asleep in the psychodrama of your mind. But if you stay present with the unfolding of the story, you will see the underlying nature of all characters — you'll see your thoughts, images, sensations, personas, and emotions — arising and disappearing on the stage of the present moment.

Again, if you let your awareness drift or if you merge with or fixate on a character, you'll become entranced in your subjectivity and miss objectivity. But if you sustain looking and seeing long enough you cannot help but to *know* what's going on. You will discover that everything on the screen of the present moment is conditioned — nothing stands alone — and therefore impermanent, insubstantial, and fundamentally unsatisfactory.

Now, if you keep looking you will see that even "knowing" is a conditioned character. And when knowing is seen through fully, this realization is nirvana — the absence of both knower and known. In other words, when the true nature of the story of consciousness is really seen as a story, one leaves the theater of knowing altogether. One wakes up out of the dream of life. These were some of the beginner's lessons offered at the monastery. I took each to heart.

A TOUCH OF LOVE

Nevertheless, the days that followed my reeducation camp were unchanged — an uneventful flow of silent nothingness on the screen of my same old sameness. Perhaps it was boredom. Or was it dullness? Maybe it was dissociation. Whatever, it didn't feel like a bad thing. It was just banal. There was even something strangely comfortable about it. There were no thoughts to speak of. There was no pain. And the only emotion I felt was this lackluster sense of awareness of not having any emotion other than a cushy feeling of mediocrity. Had I programmed myself into becoming a meditative couch potato? At times it felt as if I were stuck in a sitcom: sitting in a living room watching me on a television as the only character in a sitcom sitting in a living room looking back at me on a television.

This "Manchurian Candidate" phase of my meditation lasted about three more months. Then, one day during lunch, I noticed an elderly Burmese man sitting off to my side. He was intently focused on me as I ate my meal. Every now and again I glanced over at him and each time I was struck by his radiant features. His large brown eyes glowed with a stunning tenderness and stature. He looked to be about eighty years old. He sat calmly and confidently on the floor, with the hands placed gently on his lap, and had an elegant, solid dignity about him. His uncontrived manner was as intriguing as the subtlety of his smile. I became curious about why he was focused on me.

Midway through the meal I noticed the elder had a tear running down his cheek . . . and then another. I assumed that he must have made the food offering to us today in honor of a family member's passing, as was customary in Burma. Imagining his pain touched me and brought me out of my boredom and more into the present.

After finishing my meal I stood up, intending to return to my uneventful meditation practice, but as I did he stood up, too. He lowered his head slightly as a way of showing honor. When he lifted it up again our eyes locked. I could see the tears running down his cheeks. My heart softened. There was something so beautiful about him. I had to know why he was so sad, though, and asked, "Sir, may I ask, what makes you cry today?"

Slow to respond, he said in a gentle voice, "Oh . . . I'm happy for you, that's all. Your teacher told me that you are American. I also heard that you were the only Westerner to ordain with Mahasi Sayadaw when he went overseas in 1979, and that you've now been in the monastery a long time practicing meditation. This is rare even among our own people. And you are so young. You have such a precious opportunity to learn the Dharma. I'm honored to have been able to offer you and the other monks and nuns their meal today."

I was taken aback by his comment, and had no words to respond.

"As for me," he continued, "today I am beginning the first period of intensive meditation practice in my life. I am nearly eighty years old and have waited almost sixty years for the opportunity. As a farmer, a family man, and the headman of my village I have had a lifetime of responsibilities." He paused and motioned for the family and friends who had come to see him off to come near.

Meanwhile, the dining hall had emptied of the other monks

and nuns. Now, the elder and I were surrounded by a hundred or so radiant faces. Their love filled the space, just as the sweet smell of incense does a room.

The elder continued, saying, "We are so grateful to you. You have come so far to drink of the teachings of liberation. Thank you for your courage. We say in Burma, although one may speak beautifully about the Dharma, if one doesn't practice the teachings, it is like being a lovely flower but having no scent. Thank you for practicing these teachings. It gives us inspiration to do so ourselves."

He then placed his palms together in front of his heart, and lowering his head again, he bowed to show his respect. He and his fellow villagers then began to chant the Buddha's discourse on loving-kindness: the same chant I heard on the day I arrived a year or so before. But this time the words took on a deeper meaning. Over and over again they chanted: "May all beings be free of harm and danger. May all beings live in peace and tranquillity. May all beings be happy and harmless. May all beings realize the highest freedom."

With each refrain the words echoed through my heart, dissolving the walls of apathy and my own mediocrity — the "same old same old" that had defined my feelings for the previous three months.

I began to chant the verses on loving-kindness. In my heart I held the eyes of the elder, thinking, this wonderful man was honoring me and all that I symbolized to him about living the Dharma, yet I had been in a space without magic — a flower without a scent — for months. He was all I could ever hope to be. He was total emotion — pure presence. Just looking at him lifted me and at once my heart opened. I too had a tear in my eye.

After thanking the elder for his generosity and his kindness,

I excused myself, so as not to be late for the next scheduled meditation. But as I walked to the meditation hall I further reflected on what had just transpired with the Burmese elder. I thought about how it was one thing to be present in oneself and another thing altogether to be present in a shared moment with another. Through my meditation I had a sublime sense of stillness and suchness, but it felt deeply detached and impersonal, even narcissistic. Rather than feeling open and reverential — qualities so evident in the elder's presence — I had seemingly become impervious or immune to emotions. Was it possible to become wrongly *detached?* Did the practice of nongrasping have a shadow side, perhaps even a dark side? Was it possible to emotionally disappear in the process of discovering oneself?

From these initial questions the self-inquiry intensified. Was I really meant to spend the rest of my waking life as a renunciate, consciously forsaking the pleasures and pains of worldly living? Somehow the entire endeavor began to scare me. Instead of putting me off, however, my doubts made me redouble my efforts. Since the word Buddha literally meant "to awaken," I had to have faith in whatever came up in the process. I knew that true meditation was a "counter-egoic" process that by function often brought out the worst in people before it revealed one's deeper, more natural freedom and beauty. In the monastery this meant giving up outcome, time, history, self-identification, and any other form of normalcy until all forms of fear and attachment relaxed.

I had to have faith in the process. I had to trust my instinct for freedom. Anyway, my life in the West had been less than desirable. I had come to Burma to know a transcendent state of consciousness, ultimate truth.

At once I severed myself from further reflection and jumped

back into practice. In so doing, I brought a much more invigorated presence to the process. My sittings once again became dynamic and inspired. I got just what I needed from my encounter with the elder and now I was back in the saddle, blazing along a time-tested trail to unconditional freedom. Or so I believed.

◆ SURRENDERING TO LIFE, FULLY

After a couple of days of solid practice, with the most lucid and intimate sittings I had had in months, I was surprised to feel fatigued as I walked back to my room for the night. Not thinking anymore about it, I went to bed, looking forward to the next day's practice. When I got up in the morning, however, I had a mild headache and some nausea. Determined not to let it get me down or compromise my hard-earned meditative momentum, I took a couple of aspirins, adjusted to the nausea, and went to the hall to meditate for the day. By midafternoon the headache intensified. Thinking that a migraine was coming on I went back to my room to rest. Once down, however, I didn't get back up. That evening a fellow monk found me on my bed in a fetal position, delirious with fever, while lying in a pool of sweat, vomit, and diarrhea.

Immediately hospitalized, tests revealed both typhoid fever and cholera. From behind the blaze of a 106-degree temperature, teeth-chattering chills, vomiting, and defecating every ten minutes, I overheard the doctor tell a consul from the American embassy that "he must have eaten contaminated food" and that "he may die from the internal bleeding." I was so out of it that this news didn't matter. Nothing did. This was the closest thing to torture I had ever known. It was amazing to see the interplay of aversion and desire. Proportionate to my aversion to the pain was my craving to escape it.

Just days before I had asked U Pandita, "How does one know true enlightenment from the false one?" From the vantage point of extreme sickness, his answer made more sense than ever. "The bliss of nirvana is the most sublime form of bliss there is," he said. "But it is important to note that nirvanic bliss is not associated with the pleasures of sensory perception. How is this so, you wonder?

"Take for example, a person who is sleeping so soundly that he does not want to wake up, even if offered something pleasurable," he continued. "When that person wakes up, he says to himself, 'What a great sleep I had.'

"Now, how is it possible for one to show the pleasure that comes from deep sleep? Obviously, it's there, but it cannot be shown. And just because one cannot show it doesn't mean that it doesn't exist. Simple enough, right?

"In a similar way," he went on to say, "the presence of nirvanic bliss is not connected with the mind in any way you know it, and this bliss is many times more blissful than even the most refreshing sleep. You might say that nirvana is a bath in eternity."

He continued with increasing intensity. "More important than the bliss of nirvana is the function of it. Nirvana is the pinnacle of spiritual development. It comes when one's wisdom is thoroughly matured. From the experience one is progressively liberated from greed, anger, and delusion. Remember, without the *kilesas* — the mind's defilements — there would be no need for the Buddha's Dharma. The Buddha was a mind doctor who knew the cure for mental suffering. Forget about everything else, and focus on overcoming ignorance in this very life. The only way beyond this ignorance, and the defilements that arise from it, is the realization of nirvana."

His words never had more meaning. And only forty-eight hours had passed from months of sitting meditations in that "same old" uneventful flow of perfect nothingness. I would have traded anything to get back to that "same old" state. At the moment, my quest for nirvana had been replaced with a desire to stay alive. It was amazing to see how much attachment I had to life and how quickly my priorities could be jerked around by painful sensations.

Heavily medicated, with an IV in my arm, I stayed in bed for the next several days in a semicoma, clinging to life. Ten days later, and twenty pounds lighter, health began to return and I was able to walk again. I remember reflecting how the worst was over, and I would soon be back in the monastery, engaging in intensive meditation practice.

But destiny had a different Dharma for me. While walking to the toilet my leg gave out and I collapsed. As I did my head hit the floor and knocked me unconscious. Later that day after an examination I was told that I had a large tumor growing behind my left knee. The specialist — a Dharma student of my teacher — advised me that it would be in my best interest to have it removed.

When I woke up from surgery a day later, the doctor's face was far from relieved. As he was apologizing for a "failed operation" my heart sank. He explained how he had inadvertently sliced through the membrane that covered the knee joint in order to remove the roots of the tumor. In so doing he was unable to close the incision. As a result the knee joint fluid was seeping out of the five-inch cut he had made through the outer skin and the seepage would likely prevent everything from healing. If the incision became infected, which was likely, and if it spread into the knee joint itself, then gangrene would set in. If so, I was informed, the lower leg would have to be amputated.

Weakened into immobility from two weeks of typhoid, cholera, and now a botched operation, I lay in bed with one antibiotic drip and one saline solution drip, along with a catheter for urine, contemplating my future in the 110-degree heat. This was a strange new land in which I had no compass. The rules of life, liberation, and spiritual meaning appeared completely different. It felt like I was dying, not only physically but psychologically, too. All the ways I knew myself and could attend to myself no longer applied. I suddenly required people all the time. I was as helpless as an infant. My self-awareness was as inconsequential as a marshmallow. I had no edge, no real presence. I was given Demerol, which put me into an out-of-body *bardo* where I was both too numb to cry and too weak to care. I closed my eyes and went to sleep.

When I woke up the next day Sayadaw U Pandita was standing beside me. His warm smile was comforting. He explained how he had told his people to outfit my room in the monastery with all the medical necessities to assure my healing. After a few more days of careful observation in the hospital, I was brought back to the center, where a family of six of U Pandita's closest students, all of whom had volunteered to care for me, stayed with me in my room, around the clock.

Nonetheless, my health deteriorated. Although I was receiving beautiful care, because I was so weakened, my leg became infected. Long thick red lines, indicating infection, ran the length of my leg. The specialist insisted that he operate at once and that "the consequences could be even more drastic . . . you may lose your entire leg, and not just from the knee down." Although it made sense to follow through with a partial amputation, my instinct said no and I didn't allow it.

As a result, things got worse. In quick succession I contracted hepatitis, the flu, and amoebic dysentery. Months passed, and after losing fifty pounds I was so frail I could barely flutter my eyes. My body collapsed, fully. The consul from the American embassy came back and wanted to fly me out of the country. I shook my head in response: "No." The monastery was my home. U Pandita came to my bedside every day. Besides being my Dharma teacher, he became my father, my brother, my best friend. I had never had anyone love and engage me so intensely, compassionately, and wisely. I had not a sliver of doubt that if I were to pass away, which was possible, I wanted it to be in the monastery. It was here among my intimate Dharma friends and family that I found my life. Why not end it here too, if that was in store. By accepting the possibility of death it allowed me to surrender to life, fully.

A BED OF GRACE

I thought I had come to Burma to become liberated from suffering by not having it arise anymore, yet it was through this period of prolonged illness and pain that I was to experience a deeper happiness than I had ever known. It seemed that the more control I lost over my body, the more heightened my reverence for life became. This feeling didn't arise simply from within myself, unprompted. I was graced by the care and companionship of six loving strangers.

Although I was unable to speak very much, I bonded deeply with my voluntary caretakers. These strangers performed the most intimate functions for me: cleaning me, bathing me, taking me to the toilet, massaging my hands and feet, moistening my lips with a wet sponge, wiping the sweat from my brow, nursing me back to life by placing papaya slices in my mouth. I was cared for, deeply, in body and soul. They brought fresh flowers to my room. They read discourses of the Buddha to me and a few of Mahasi Sayadaw's books that had been translated into English. Hearing the spoken Dharma relaxed my heart. It opened me to a whole new realm of shared presence, whereby the idea of the individual was transcended and replaced by an interactive, mutual meditation that was as intimate and real as being kissed. For hours they would sit quietly on the floor either reading or meditating. They chanted at night to put me to sleep. Their sanctity filled me and the room with a grace that made me feel that it was almost worth getting this sick just to see the Dharma so profoundly expressed.

I was a vulnerable child in the hands of caring strangers. It is rare for any of us to remember the unconditional love our parents gave to us as babies. These loving hands gave me a rare glimpse back into my own infancy as well as a preview of what old age may look like. It is remarkably rare to witness any form of unconditional care, whether it be compassion, love, generosity, or basic kindness. I felt blessed.

These months of illness and care touched me more profoundly than any meditative insight. Perhaps the practice itself allowed me to receive and feel the intimacy and beauty showered upon me night and day. I'll never know. What I was given was a clear and compelling example of what "engaged presence" looks like. This was what kindness, caring, and generosity look like when freely expressed. These lovely people gave me my first real sense of finding liberation through living.

Not once did my caretakers complain or flinch from the filth of my bodily fluids. Their steady tenderness awakened beauty in me. I recognized just how fragile we are, and that I wasn't just some empty process turned onto the Dharma. From a taste of my humanness a bliss arose, not born from meditative concentration or from a flash of insight but from a recognition of the pure poignancy of being a fragile human lying on my "bed of grace." I went to sleep many nights during this time with a smile on my face. For all the physical pain, it was a stunning experience.

From my bed of grace I realized that there were many highly enhanced states of consciousness, including nirvana, that I did not know. There may well be a state of suspended animation, beyond the mind itself, but why seek such a state when one is always present with infinite mystery? I was *searching* for a state of nonsearching. Such a thought had never dawned on me before this deeply. I think I was so busy as a dedicated Buddhist practitioner, trying to transform primordial ignorance before I died, that I missed the innate beauty of my ordinary humanity.

When I took the agenda out of being present, I was left with this moment, now. And what else do we have but this breath, right now? As I settled more into this realization even my most sacred spiritual identities began to vanish — being a Buddhist, a monk, a meditator, a renunciate, a celibate, a moral person, or even a person seeking liberation — leaving just this sense of an ordinary, natural being relating to the presence around me. Meditation became the living practice of dying into being. If a moral order to the cosmos existed I didn't know it. I had thought that I would only get enlightened by sitting still in meditation, but something was coming through as I lay flat on my back with three tubes in my arm. Since I figured I might die at any moment, why would I want to compromise myself with spiritual superficiality?

It was here that I began to drop my learned religious references. Even the Dharma disappeared. It became obvious that the present moment wasn't a strategic stepping-stone to walk across toward some idealized freedom in the future. Being present was simply its own reward — ordinary, poetic, banal, stunning, wild, eerie, erotic, dumb, careless, brilliant. And all I could see as I lay there wasting away physically was that presence was an invitation to fullness, a space of being pregnant with both the creative and diabolical forces of the universe.

Slowly I came back to life. Six months passed. My leg healed. My illnesses were cured. I regained energy. I could walk again. Life had never felt sweeter. The bounce in my step that I had as a teenager returned. It took almost dying to stop trying to escape life and to get on with the beauty of being.

I was so jazzed that I decided that I had enough meditation

for awhile. Despite Sayadaw U Pandita's admonishment, in which he reminded me to "fulfill my real reason for coming to Burma and free the mind of all forms of delusion," I opted to begin a study of the classical Buddhist texts under the guidance of an English-speaking Burmese Buddhist scholar.

One day, nine months after contracting typhoid and cholera, I was walking through the monastery on my way to class. As I was hustling along I heard someone call out my monk's name, Aggacara. Since I was late for the class I didn't stop. Then I heard my name again. When I heard my name a third time my conscience got the best of me. I stopped, turned, and stood waiting for two Burmese men I didn't know to walk up to me. Running through my head was the thought, "Come on . . . to the point please . . . I'm late."

They walked up and smiled but said nothing. This annoyed me slightly but I didn't show it. Instead, in a slightly brusque tone, I asked, "Yes, what is it?"

The younger Burmese man replied, "I'm so happy to see that you're better." Both men were beaming. I thought "Okay, come on guys. You knew I was sick, but everyone in the monastery knew that." I asked, "Do I know you?"

"Yes," he said with a warm smile, "I'm one of those who took care of you when you were dying." He motioned to the elder man and said, "This is my father. He told me that you met when he began his retreat last year."

I was mortified. How could I forget this man's face or the face of his father?

Sensing my uneasiness, he said, "You must be going somewhere important. We're just happy that you're healthy again. Please, excuse us, we must be going ourselves." The two men placed their hands reverentially in front of their hearts, graciously lowered their heads, then backed away, and left.

As I stood there watching them leave the monastery, I collapsed into the depth of love I felt for them both. I also saw how fragile my understanding of the Dharma was. After a year of intensive meditation, nine months of illness, and thirty years of life, I could still stand in this spot and address these wonderful men with impatience. From the disgrace I felt toward myself the passion of *sanvega* began to ignite. I realized that I must look more deeply into those hidden areas of myself to discover a way of being that was not only more present and available, but less driven by egotistic pride. Nirvana called to me once again. I felt compelled to return to the reason I came to Burma — to explore the nature of consciousness through intensive meditation so as to come to the end of suffering.

A TRUE SPIRITUAL FRIEND

That evening I put away my books and again entered intensive meditation, committing myself to silence and the twenty-hour-a-day schedule. The meditation evolved naturally. I was excited to be back in retreat. I was encouraged by U Pandita "to be smooth... foster a gentle presence" and "be guided by an understanding of the middle way — neither accepting or rejecting anything."

It became clear, once again, that in a world where the only constant was change, attaching to anything was pure folly. Without clinging, meditation was a ride, inherently empty, and free of right and wrong. Here, despite the tentative insights brought to me by my illness of a Dharma without a goal, the aspiration to experience nirvana — the transcendent zero point of pure consciousness — began to take root all over again.

When I explained my "desire to experience the unspeakable" to Sayadaw U Pandita, emphasizing how happy I was to finally get the importance of meditation practice and being in long-term intensive retreat, he acknowledged my passion with a nod, saying simply, "carry on." As I was leaving his cottage, I was feeling somewhat disappointed that "my needs were not met." Just as I was opening the door, I heard his voice: "Be watchful of formulating opinions. Freedom is beyond form. Remember your illness?" He wanted to make sure that I understood that he wasn't there to give me approval as much as he was to mirror my ego.

I nodded my yes, acknowledging his wisdom and compassion.

He went on to say, "It's not helpful to think of being in retreat or out of retreat, practicing or not practicing. As a monk your life is about awareness, that's all. And this awareness is not bound up with concepts of time, place, or circumstance.

"When you get up from a sitting meditation, be watchful of the thought 'my sitting has ended.' Dissolve this notion of beginning and ending, starting and stopping. Comparison is an illusion. There is no absolute to compare to. Although we have clocks, there is no real time, there is no night and day for a meditator. Your only task is to be aware of the reality of being in the moment as it arises, on the surface of your mind. Look at it . . . see it . . . know it . . . and you will be free."

Reflecting on this, I asked, "But aren't retreats indispensable? Don't we need to be in intensive meditation to liberate ourselves from misperceptions about the nature of consciousness? I certainly didn't see this quality of awakening happening in my daily life."

"Consciousness is the Dharma. It is wherever you are. Living the Dharma should be understood as a way of being, awake and present," he said. "We have many cases here in Burma of people 'finding liberation' without being in retreat. Their life is the Dharma, a dedication to paying close attention to their motivations, their thoughts, their state of mind, the way they walk and move about. Mangoes fall when they're ripe. Wisdom ripens at a different pace and a different way for everyone. But one truth remains . . . it is awareness that liberates the mind, not a form or a doctrine. The Buddha made this clear, saying 'a true monk or nun is not one who has renounced the world, but one who has renounced fear, grasping, and delusion.'

"As I said, have no conclusions about anything. Wisdom evolves based upon openness, sincerity, and self-honesty. It has nothing to do with how long you can or cannot sit in meditation. It has nothing to do with how many retreats you have done. Wisdom is beyond all ideas and forms. What's important is the willingness to look at yourself. Equal to that is your honesty with me. Say only what you know from direct experience. Now, please carry on."

Over time my relationship with Sayadaw U Pandita became a source of incomparable subtlety and wonder. He was without a doubt the finest person I had ever met. As my teacher he treated me not as a student, but as a son. Not only did I learn the complexities of the Dharma with him, but I felt like I was re-parented by him as well. It was nothing short of true love, born from within the context of liberation. He consistently brought both a tenderness to the tough times and a tireless ability to laugh and play. At sixty years old he was still a boy. Yet if necessary he would get in a cage with a tiger. He had spiritual warrior running through his veins. As such he had no mercy for my ignorance. Nor did I ever find him the slightest bit patronizing or concerned with coddling my ego. To the contrary he seemed to do what he did without any need for reward or applause. With the sensitivity of a surgeon he would help me lift back the veils of self-deception. Sometimes he could do it by merely remaining silent. At other times he shot an arrow through my bubble with a glance or a stare.

He had compassion, helping untangle my ego knots and other forms of self-fixation with straight-ahead directness. Personas and mental postures were not encouraged. He considered *Dharma mana,* or spiritual pride, to be the main reason for stagnation in the Dharma and in meditation. He believed that clinging on to a false idea of one's "spiritual depth" or "enlightenment experiences" was the largest obstacle of all.

If he thought you were being dumb he would say it. If you thought you were enlightened and you wanted to run your "peak experience" by him, he'd be frank and tell you what he thought. He offered me the most compassionate, dignified, and authentic style of relationship I had ever known. And as far as I could see he wanted nothing from me except my sincere effort to listen, to question, to reason, to be free.

As the retreat unfolded, my heart burst open with inspiration. Like a rainbow, consciousness was seen as a spectrum of endless nuances. When I shared this understanding, he responded by saying, "This is known as meditative *piti* — the joy associated with Dharma inquiry. It functions to enliven the seven qualities of liberation: awareness, intuition, energy, gladness, composure, concentration, and balance. When these qualities of consciousness mature, the mind opens as naturally as a flower does to the sun. We call this the flowering of the Dharma, and its fragrance is freedom."

"Although intensive meditation is a solo affair, it shouldn't be done alone," U Pandita once said. "At least not until one is proficient in one's understanding of the seven qualities of liberation." With this in mind, he showed me how intensive meditation practice was essentially a temporary marriage between oneself and one's guide. The Buddha called this role *kalayanamitta* — a true spiritual friend — and once declared that it was indispensable to the awakening of wisdom.

My daily sessions with U Pandita were my time to see a masterful *kalayanamitta* in action. Although I was asked to "explain only the most interesting ten minutes of the previous twenty-four hours of meditation practice," our daily sessions, often exceeding an hour, were considered a continuation of the retreat, and not a time off from them. From the moment I walked into his cottage until the very moment I walked out the door, he asked me to "be aware of every nuance of your being as if they were your last acts on earth."

He considered the dialogue that we had together to be an "interactive meditation" purposely designed to reveal the terrain of his students' consciousness, providing him with the subtle and gross elements of their day-to-day awakening. Those "peak ten minutes" you chose to explore could be about anything: your peak pain, your peak pleasure, your peak peace, your peak anger, your peak drivel, your peak wisdom — anything. It was up to you. He would listen, question, dialogue, question, and then ask you if you had a question. After it was over he'd jot down a few words in his notebook to remind himself of where you were, and then you would go.

During my early years in Burma, before other Westerners started to come, he would repeat this process with one hundred or more Burmese meditators every day, each for five minutes. Essentially, his role was to observe the meditator's progress and keep you on track, with or without you knowing it.

Although he saw freedom as a goal, he also saw it as both an isolated event in the moment as well as a process that evolved over time. He was never the least bit pushy about reaching some expected outcome, asking, rather, that one maintain the integrity of the moment. He once admonished me to be watchful of the habit of "being aware in order to *get* free." This was subtle stuff. "Freedom is the absolute absence of wanting," he would say. "Nirvana is never greedy," he once said in a laughing tone.

"You take yourself to the doorway of nirvana, but to go in you must stay at the entrance. That's why nirvana literally means the 'extinguishing of desire.' It is the absolute absence of 'being for or against anything.'"

ENTERING THE STREAM OF LIBERATION

Early into this next phase of retreat U Pandita explained, "There are two types of liberation: momentary and sustained. When you string together many moments of momentary nirvana, consciousness matures. Once wisdom is fully ripened, consciousness enters the unconditioned state of nirvana, a taste of unconditioned freedom.

"This taste of the unconditioned transforms the stream of one's consciousness irrevocably, liberating it from a certain level of ignorance permanently.

"Further, when one comes out of the unconditioned, liberation remains present. From this point on we say that one has entered the 'stream of liberation.' It is a current that brings consciousness along as naturally as a river flows into the ocean.

"Since both types of freedom are born from 'being present,' you will see that there is no logic in pursuing long-term liberation — or the unconditioned nirvana — when the only way to that freedom is through awareness of the present moment right now.

"Remember, to practice freedom, neither let your mind wander outside, nor let it stop inside. Neither wish to end suffering nor long for happiness. When one breath leaves the body be watchful of wanting it to return. Be willing to live and die in each moment. This freedom is beyond stillness. Beyond duration. Beyond fixation. Beyond perceiver and perceived. Just be slow and steady. Be relaxed and alert at the same time."

As my meditation evolved our Dharma sessions intensified. Rather than a teacher and a student, it often felt like one mind interrelating with itself. As awareness gathered momentum, the insight into impermanence and insubstantiality matured. As it did, tranquillity disappeared and was replaced by a loathing toward the inherent futility of conditioned existence. Playing the yearning and avoiding game made no sense when every perception burst like a bubble. Bodies seemed like fleshy holograms that bled, oozed, and devoured for survival. Life was a prison of knowing. No spin could make this perception of disgust any less tormenting. At this point I gave up hope and faith and an array of stashed-away strategies for my glorious plans to help save the world once I was liberated and returned to the West.

As these perceptions peaked, and my sense of hopelessness descended into gloom, I was convinced that no place inside or outside was safe. There was no asylum anywhere. It had been easier to witness this truth about the outer world, but to see that bliss and beauty themselves were conditioned phantoms — tricks within consciousness — and therefore dangerous, was another thing altogether. In a momentary lapse, ignorance could jerk you into the trance of thought, and there, fused within a synthetic creation, one would live in the coma of conceptualization. This perception made me tremble with fear.

I never knew what spiritual longing meant until I reached this stage. Or, I should say, spiritual loathing. I craved one thing: liberation from perception — the *nonarising* of any formation whatsoever within consciousness. From a worldly view this might have sounded like escapism, but from my vantage point it was nothing less than running out of a house that was on fire. I concluded that knowledge of any sort was fire — *dukkha,* suffering. I wanted to know the transcendent mind that ceased knowing the "world as I knew it." Whatever nirvana was, I wanted to abide in it, irrevocably.

Awakening in the Dharma had turned ugly. As I was going

through this stage, the old adage "ignorance is bliss" took on poignant meaning. I was convinced that meditation had ruined my life. Not surprisingly, this made me feel deeply ambivalent about my search for nirvana. I couldn't decide what to do. It was completely overwhelming. I remember the day I went to my session with Sayadaw U Pandita ready to pack it in. I told him, "I want to cease being a slave to consciousness. I want to escape this prison of knowing." He was cool and showed no enthusiasm for my aspiration. Unexpectedly, rather than giving me some subtle Dharma teaching, he suggested that I sweep the path outside my cottage, take a bath, and come back to his place after lunch for cake and ice cream. I did just that, in addition to smoking a cigar I bummed from one of the groundskeepers.

After lunch I returned to his cottage. We sat on the floor around a small table and ate fruit, small cakes, and ice cream together in silence. His calm and graceful manner soothed my perception of disgust and loathing and, for the first time in days, my mind became calm enough to gather some insight. I began to reflect more objectively on the state of my mind. The idea of ending my retreat scared me as much as continuing it. But something stirred from within. I am simply seeing the nature of the mind, I reflected. I'm seeing the mind unfiltered through beliefs, faith, and fantasies. Trust reality I told myself. Trust your instinct for freedom — your deepest sense of truth and dignity. See these perceptions as projections through the lens of fear and disgust that are contorting me. Don't run from them but see them for what they are. If I stop practice, this level of awareness will cease. The mind will slow and blur again. Reality will become masked. Concepts will camouflage reality and I will be lured back into forms. I will resume longing and avoiding, hoping and fearing.

Once entangled in society again I may never escape. It is a miracle that I'm in Burma at this time, blessed with a Dharma teacher, with food, shelter, and health. The time is now, I concluded. Walk out of your confusion. Choose radical liberation, not ordinary comfort. Press on I said to myself. Renew your courage, and get on with it. I lowered my fork and bowed to my teacher saying, "time to go back to it."

He smiled and said, "It gets sweeter as you go on." We held each other's eyes for a few moments. His sensitivity touched me deeply. As I held his smile I let his love suffuse me, nurture me, and inspire me to carry on. I wiped a tear from my eye and left the room so appreciative of his heart to stay with me in this process of understanding the Dharma — the nature of my own mind.

The moment heralded a new beginning. As I walked to the meditation hall to resume practice, I was filled with gratitude. This insight wasn't a curse but a blessing. It seemed I had been cleansed of certain misperceptions about life. Yes, life was impermanent; it was also insubstantial and unable to satisfy the needs of a lasting happiness. But so what? That's life. That's truth. Truth was preferable to illusion. This understanding brought a dignity with it. Such is suchness. It is as it is. I smiled back into the process, and carried on.

A few days later my practice reached new heights. Two-hour sittings blinked by in what felt like twenty minutes. I was neither elated nor dismayed by anything. The mind was frictionless, free of fixation, and effortlessly present without the slightest reference to an observer or an observed. It felt like a pure transparent flow of referenceless presence.

U Pandita's only instruction was this: "Make no special effort. Be natural. Follow your own rhythm. Just keep filling in the gaps of unawareness."

For the next week I did just that. And as I did, my meditative awareness refined and became smoother. It got to the place where I felt that I would be enlightened at any moment. I could stay here for eternity, I thought. But that would not be my fate.

THERE IS NO TIME OFF FROM FREEDOM

I had thought my illness had prepared me for the unexpected. "Why is someone knocking on my door?" I wondered. Slowly I changed my posture and got up from my sitting. Opening the door, I could see by the blank expression on the staff member's face that something was up. I took the note and read: "Authorities in the government informed us today that you must leave Burma at once. No reason was given. Please come to the office immediately and we will book you a flight for tomorrow morning." I stood there stunned and motionless.

Thinking there must be a mistake, I put on my upper robe and raced to the front office to investigate. The president of the monastery made it clear that things were not negotiable. "We live under dictatorship," he said. "We have no rights and we have no recourse."

"But why me? Why do I have to leave?" I asked.

"They're a xenophobic government," he replied.

"Nothing can be done?" I inquired, searching for hope.

"I'm sorry," he said. "It's not in my control."

The finality in his words paralyzed me into silence.

He then said, "We'll be happy to buy you a ticket. Where would you like to go?"

The thought was utterly foreign. For the previous two years my home had been this monastery. Burma was my Shangri-la, my salvation — the only place I had ever felt at home. My primary activity had been silent meditation — evolving a presence beyond location, time, and conceptualization. Now I was forced to decide my entire future on the spot.

"I know this comes as a shock. Perhaps you'd like to think about it for an hour or so?"

"No," I said, coming back to reality. "I'll go to Calcutta. I was there some years ago. Why not?"

His face twisted into an expression of surprise and he asked, "You don't want to return to America?"

I recoiled. There was no way I would go back to the West. It would be my death, I thought. My reaction was enough of an answer. "Okay," he said. "The flight to Calcutta usually has space. Come to the office after breakfast tomorrow and we'll take you to the airport."

I thanked him for his generous support and left for U Pandita's cottage to explain the situation to him. He was saddened but encouraging. "The world will make you stronger," he said in his characteristically calm, strong tone. "You'll have a good chance to put the meditation into action."

After a few more words we both went silent. The quiet quickly filled with the sorrow of separation — I was being taken away from my cherished teacher and my best friend. He had been my life link. He was simply the best companion I had ever known. I had never known that I was capable of so much attachment until this moment.

U Pandita asked everyone in the room to leave and he spoke to me as a father to a son. I cried uncontrollably. After a long talk he concluded by saying, "Awareness is the true teacher. In the world, this awareness will bring you out of yourself and situate you very close to the hearts of others. This will pose a great challenge to you. There are four things to remember in bringing the Dharma into the world: bring love, compassion, honor, and poise to each person you meet. Learn from your shortcomings, and try not to judge others for their weaknesses. Elevate yourself with goodness. Learn to transmute fear with courage, anger with love, greediness with generosity. Bring hope to people. Reveal the Dharma by being the Dharma. Above all, be aware. There is no time off from freedom. Don't leave your breath in the monastery. This is how a true monk brings meditation into the world." His guidance was the light in my life. I bowed to my beloved teacher and left, not knowing if we would ever meet again.

The following morning, I paid my respects to Mahasi Sayadaw and asked him for any advice he might offer. "Do all that you can in this life to know your mind," he said. "All that you will ever need to know is already there — within you. Know the mind and you will know liberation."

I thanked him for providing me with the greatest opportunity of my life. I bowed to my preceptor and left the room.

OUR PRESENCE IS ALL WE HAVE

So, with my begging bowl, a sitting cloth, a shaving razor, and a passport, I flew across the Bay of Bengal on a one-way ticket to Calcutta. I had no idea what I would do. I had no money. As a monk I was not allowed to even touch it. Oddly, I felt safe, protected, and strangely secure. I took refuge in the reality that our presence is all that we have.

And so began the next leg of my Dharma odyssey. A few hours later I stepped off the plane in Calcutta. Eighteen hours before I was what felt like a hair's breadth from enlightenment and now I was walking into a city of eleven million people, dodging rickshaws. Traffic spewed exhaust through intersections stuffed wall to wall with people, while cows, goats, and dogs nipped at my robes and heels.

After a free bus ride I got out and walked across the Howrah Bridge — the gateway to the city. Entering Calcutta at any hour is like entering a surreal humanscape of samsaric carnage: legs and arms unimaginably twisted and bent, or missing; beggars squatting, lying, and dying in the gutters; others sleeping against walls, oblivious to the death and squalor all around them; entire communities of families living in scrap-wood boxes covered with plastic or cardboard. Under the ramps, along the riverbanks, in every conceivable square foot of earth and pavement were people, barely clinging to life. Calcutta is raw and exposed, undoubtedly one of the great, unmasked windows into the dark heart of reality. With running water often limited to two thirty-minute periods a day, and with electricity blackouts up to eight hours at a time, sometimes five days a week, it's hard to imagine that it all kept going, but it did.

I kept walking, passing exotic markets and shops with magnificent embroidered fabrics and gorgeous women in their colorful saris. Beyond the filth I noticed flowers everywhere. Almost every shop had a vase full and almost every woman had some in her hair.

There were old mansions built by the British. Some had chauffeur-driven cars parked in front of them, while groups of beggars groped and knocked on their blackened windows hoping for a face of compassion.

Magnificent temples were as plentiful as cathedrals in France. Each had its pantheon of statues of every variation and size, dedicated to every Hindu god and deity there ever was.

As I continued walking I encountered a number of lepers whose hands had been reduced to bloody, festering nubs. Their presence touched me. I asked myself if I could manifest the same quality of kindness that my own caretakers showed me when I was ill. I couldn't help thinking what it would have been like for me not to have been cared for.

As I walked on with one leper's hand in my face, I reflected on a time when Sayadaw U Pandita explained to me that "if you want to develop compassion you have to make the suffering of another your own. Allow your heart to quiver. Allow it to be touched. To open!"

"Before you turn away," he said, "put yourself in their body, their mind, and pause. Feel their condition as your own. If fear arises, challenge it. If disgust arises, challenge it too. Challenge any thought that tells you it's wrong or that it is too much. Remain determined in your effort. You must see the situation as opportunity — for your own liberation and their happiness, too. Then ask yourself, What can be done to ease this person's pain, their struggle? What act can you do to help?"

"Compassion," he went on to say, "cannot be considered complete by merely feeling the suffering of another as one's own. Compassion must be accompanied by action. Compassion is a behavior, not just a thought."

Fighting my own fear and revulsion, I turned to look directly at the face of the leper beside me. For a moment before he moved away, we shared a breath of existence together.

Now that I was abruptly back in the world, my teacher's explanation of compassion became a guiding principle. This brought greater clarity to the Buddha's encouragement to make each person you meet the most sacred place for spiritual awakening, for without other people, liberation would not be possible.

A few hours later, after it had become dark, I came across a child, perhaps only eight years old. She was carrying what looked like a dead infant in her arms — eyes begging, hungry — her outstretched hand was in desperate search of a few pennies. I'd seen some pretty terrible sights before, but nothing quite like this. She just stood there. Our eyes locked. I had no money. After a few moments I reached into my shoulder bag, pulled out a piece of palm sugar, which I carried with me to quiet the hunger, and placed it in her hand. Instantly her fingers grasped tightly around it. Expressionless, she ran off as the infant's arms dangled in the air like a doll.

I walked on, stunned, wondering, Who was this God, this great intelligence emanating totality, that allowed the poverty, disease, and suffering I saw everywhere around me? Why is the world like this? What determines our fate?

Samsara spews forth existence in a continuous display of mind-boggling variation. Perhaps the *why* is unknowable. Is it random? Is it some lawful chaotic karmic symmetry? Or is life really a dream, like so many holy people would like us to believe, and our only salvation is to wake up, and wake again and again until we've unveiled the last illusion of separate identity? Is it true that life is a holographic emptiness? In that case is horror just God's cosmic play to wake his or her children up?

I don't think I had ever really questioned my motives for embracing a spiritual life, beyond overcoming my own suffering, until I walked as a monk into Calcutta. It was here that I felt the impact of asking, "What does really matter, and why?"

THE WEIRDNESS OF EVERYDAY LIFE

I stayed a few months in Calcutta, living on the street in the Kali Ghat area of the city, near the Black Hole, where the poorest of the poor lived. I chose the area because it was near Mother Teresa's Center for the Destitute and Dying. At first I thought I might help out but opted for the weirdness of everyday life on the street instead. After some adjustments I blended right in. I slept outside, often sitting up against a wall all night. I had learned the technique in Burma from an old monk who hadn't slept lying down for fifty years. It was surprising how restful it was.

As a monk, the locals generously brought me food and rice. In the evenings I would often chant with the local Hindu holy men sitting around a campfire. Occasionally I'd visit Mother Teresa's center, but for the most part I preferred to stay on my own. Most nights were spent at the local burning *ghat,* where I would peer into the flames for hours, watching as a body was cremated in any one of the dozens of fires that raged around the clock. The experience was sobering. It disabused me of a certain attraction and attachment to form, appearances, and flesh. One moment these people were alive and in the next they were dead. Just like that, in an instant, life was severed and came to an end. This proximity to death was freeing.

Overall, my time in Calcutta was interesting. In some ways I felt more liberated on the street than I did in meditation in the monastery. There was something so weirdly pure and organic about it. No clocks. No schedule. No contrivances at all. With so much death and poverty all around, life was raw and unmasked. This touched me deeply.

One morning I was stopped by an American couple. Once they realized I was a Westerner, their faces piqued with curiosity and they greeted me with an enthusiastic *namaste,* a Hindu greeting that means I honor the God in you as the same God in me. The man startled me with a piercing and shiftless gaze. I was amazed at how irritated I became. How easy it was to love a beggar, I thought, especially in comparison to a self-assured, wealthy, overly spiritualized American stranger.

After telling him that "as a Buddhist I don't do eye," he backed off, apologized, and introduced himself and his girlfriend. Both of them had Hindu god names, similar to Ram Dass, the former Harvard professor who wrote the book *Be Here Now.* In fact, they may have been from that same spiritual scene. A portrait of a large bald Indian man wrapped in a blanket dangled from the *mala* beads they wore as necklaces.

The man proceeded to explain how they were lost and needed directions on how to get to Mother Teresa's Center for the Destitute and Dying. As I was giving them instructions, we naturally began to chat about ourselves. We were, after all, fellow Americans, living in a foreign land.

He gleefully shared how they owned a home in Mill Valley — an affluent town just across the Golden Gate Bridge north of San Francisco. Although they didn't say it, they looked to be in their early forties. She said they were both psychotherapists with Ph.D.'s in clinical psychology, each with a large private practice. They did yoga, ate vegan, and kept journals. They were both articulate and good-looking. And they both looked like they had been in India for some time. He had a scraggly beard, wore

Indian-style white clothing, a vest, and Birkenstocks with socks. She wore a Tibetan dress with dozens of silver bangles on both arms and a small diamond stud through her nose.

I must have looked even weirder to them than they did to me. I was bald, in orange robes, and barefoot. And I'm sure they were judging me as much as I was judging them. The only difference may have been that I felt justified in my judgment of them whereas they had nothing on me. At least I was authentic, I told myself. They were just looking the part. Although I didn't realize it at the time, I think we judge in others that which we either deny or dislike in ourselves. After a while he explained how they had been in India for about a year "looking for the real thing."

"We just got fed up with the West Coast spiritual scene," he said. "Been there done that." She nodded sympathetically in agreement.

"What's wrong with it?" I asked curiously. "It's been about two years since I've been there."

"You're not missing anything," he replied, carving a look of disgust.

"Yeah . . . we've tried it all," she said.

"We did 'breath work.' Why pay a lot of money to hyperventilate and cry your way through a cathartic circus act?" he asked rhetorically.

"Too much Mommy-Daddy stuff," she said with a smirk.

"We also did primal scream. They should update their work a bit," he said sarcastically.

"Did *vipassana,* too. Hard work. Strange too! Here we were expected to sit still in meditation all day and the guy leading the retreat is never in the meditation hall himself. Seemed more like a gig to him than anything sacred."

"Now our psychoanalysis was good. Some real deep stuff came out." She nodded in agreement.

"More recently," he said, "we've had some private sessions with a great guide, using MDMA — Ecstasy. Amazing stuff."

"You ever use it?" he asked. "We've got some if you want it."

"What's it do?" I asked.

"It brings you into the now... and opens your heart too," she said with a warm smile as if transfixed by the memory.

"Not just that," he added, "it brings you in close to the truth of who you are beneath your denial and defenses. It's been the most important therapeutic opening tool I've ever come across."

"Then again," he said, pausing in a moment of reflection, "the healing process has just begun." They both looked at each other and nodded in agreement.

Healing process, I thought to myself. What are they talking about? Are they ill? I had never heard the word "healing" used in a spiritual context. It confused me.

"I don't mean to intrude, but are you both sick?" I asked cautiously, but seriously.

Startled by the question, she spoke up. "No, of course not. Why do you ask? Do we look sick?"

"You just said you were both in a healing process. I thought maybe you were ill." I was thoroughly confused.

They looked at each other and laughed. "No, we're not sick," she said. "What he meant was that we've both uncovered a lot of past hurts. Old wounds, you know, traumas from childhood. We're in the process of healing them — working them through."

"See, I had an extremely unavailable father, and he had a very controlling mother. It's been a long battle trying to overcome their influence."

"Frankly, he still gets attracted to other women," she said as if fighting a rancid memory. "Let me tell you... we've had our rounds on this issue. He can't seem to integrate his *anima*."

Rather than reacting he twisted a smile and said, "Oh... that doesn't happen anymore. But still, it's part of who I am. I've told you all along. What do you expect me to do, just turn that part of me off and pretend that you are the only girl who turns me on?"

"What did you say?" she tossed back. "Are you trying to impress the monk?"

"Can't bear the truth?" he asked. "I thought you were committed to the process?"

At that moment a leper walked up to us. Asking for money, he held up his arm to show us the pulpy stump of hand where his fingers used to be. She was so infuriated that she was oblivious to the leper. "You asshole. You always make it sound like I'm attacking you. You speak about your need for assertiveness and autonomy, and the truth is you hide behind your rhetoric. You're a spiritual fraud."

How interesting, I thought to myself. I like that term. It had never dawned on me that I may be one too. Suddenly my interest was stirred.

"Fraud, my ass," he said.

As they shouted back and forth the beggar continued to ask for a few coins, saying, "You have everything, I have nothing, a few *pisa* [pennies] please."

"You always do this to me," she yelled. "And now in public, too!"

"And me? I'm never enough for you . . . just being me," he retaliated.

Meanwhile, I stood there judging them for being oblivious to the beggar and thinking how they both need to get into long-term meditation, if someone would have them.

Suddenly the man turned from his girlfriend and shouted at the beggar, "Go away!"

Looking back at her, he says, "Look what you've done."

"I haven't done anything. I'm just being myself. Screw you."

As the beggar walked away she turned to me and in an apologetic tone said, "We're really sorry about this."

"Yeah, truly," he said. "Anyway, you were saying . . . which is the way to Mother Teresa's?"

As they walked off I thanked them both in my mind for giving me the gift of being more aware of the "consciousness raising" movement sweeping American culture, a movement that would soon begin to invade Asia. My encounter with the Americans had been upsetting on a number of levels and it emboldened me to isolate myself even further.

THE SERENDIPITY OF DESTINY

A few days later a local bus driver invited me to come along with him down the coast to the south. He fixed a spot on the roof for me and off we went. A day later I got off in Madras. From there I found a local Buddhist center and stayed the night.

A couple of days later, the patrons of the center generously bought me a one-way ticket to Sri Lanka — the small country off the tip of southern India. Once there, I walked south along the coast about seventy miles to find a monastery Mahasi Sayadaw had once told me about called the Island Hermitage — a one-hundred-year-old Buddhist monastery located on a ten-acre island in the middle of a large lagoon. The monastery had been founded in the late 1800s by Nyanatiloka — a German monk — and then later taken over by his student Nyanaponika, also a German. Mahasi Sayadaw had once explained that Nyanaponika had practiced intensive meditation at his center in Rangoon back in the 1950s. Nyanaponika went on to become one of the most respected Western Buddhist monks of our era, writing *The Heart of Buddhist Meditation.* It is the first and perhaps best book ever written on insight (*vipassana*) meditation as taught by Mahasi Sayadaw. In addition to its natural beauty, the hermitage housed one of the best English-language Buddhist libraries in Asia.

I spent the next year alone in Nyanatiloka's old cliff-top

cottage. My life was simple and remote, without running water, flush toilets, or electricity. Unlike Calcutta, life on a tropical jungle island was anything but impoverished. Also, as a living member of the food chain, I saw that it was anything but romantic. I came to see the true nature of nature. It is vicious. In the jungle everything ate something all of the time. Owls ate the mice. Bats ate the insects. Snakes ate the rats. Frogs ate the flies. Mosquitoes ate us. We ate the fish. Fish ate the smaller fish. The worms ate the leftovers. Death was birth's inheritance. The island was like a huge mouth eating its own body.

I remember seeing a five-foot, one-hundred-pound iguana-like lizard attempt to swallow an injured eight footer. Unable to swallow it, the two reptiles remained locked together, thrashing in pain for a week, until thousands of ants ate them alive from the inside out. Not only did the ants feast, but every other creature got in on it, too. The crows pecked the lizards. Even baby lizards came in for their piece. The experience confirmed my teacher's words: "*Samsara* eats itself to stay alive... and you question why the Buddha taught an escape from *samsara?*"

At the end of 1981 I had a series of dreams in which Sayadaw U Pandita was talking to me, calling me back to the monastery to continue my meditation practice. This appealed to me but I had no idea if I would be allowed to reenter the country. Nor did I have money for a ticket. A few days later my dear friend Louise Lamontagne, who worked at the Canadian embassy in the capital city, Colombo, came to the monastery for an unexpected visit. She said that she was having dreams of me going back to Burma. She was curious if I had any interest in returning. After saying yes, she kindly offered to buy a ticket. I expressed my deep gratitude for her timely support, to which she said, "No... it's my pleasure. Thank you for the opportunity to give."

Until Louise's passing away from liver cancer in 2001, at

fifty-one, she playfully referred to herself as "Alan's first Dharma student." I, on the other hand, live with the memory of her beauty and remarkable generosity, while blessed to be the godfather to her only child, Cory.

After receiving a seven-day visa in a stopover, I reentered Burma. And without a glitch the regime granted me a long-term extension. As easily as I got in the first time, it happened again. But this time I was more aware of the fragility of my circumstances.

It was a profound joy to be reunited with Sayadaw U Pandita. Taking nothing for granted, I dove immediately back into my meditation practice. To my surprise, over the next nine months my meditation never reached the depth that it had before. Essentially, it was a period of maturing sustained awareness, simply being in the flow of being — neither boring nor interesting. One day a staff member from the front office came knocking on my door again, with the same message as before: "the authorities want you out of the country."

At this point, I went to Australia at the invitation of my dear friend Joseph Goldstein, a founder of the Insight Meditation Society in Massachusetts. The plan was to co-teach a couple of Dharma retreats. Joseph and I had remained close from the time we first met at Naropa in the summer of 1974. But after co-teaching the retreats, I realized that what I most wanted to do was return to Burma, to be with my teachers and continue practicing meditation. I went to the Burmese embassy in Canberra and asked for their help. For some reason luck was on my side and I was given permission, yet again, to reenter Burma.

Joseph generously bought me a ticket and within days I was back settling once again into the meditation practice, more determined than ever not to let the opportunity slip from my hands. I wanted to know that place beyond time, beyond conditions, beyond anything I had ever known. I had learned a lot about the nature of the mind at this point, but I still did not know the unconditioned — the elusive bliss of nirvana. If it existed this was my moment to see for myself the heart essence of the Buddha's teachings.

AWARENESS LIBERATES, NOT THE DESIRE FOR FREEDOM

It was at this stage that my practice clicked. Through several weeks of a *sanvega*-inspired awareness, along with a more supple concentration than ever before, the mind moved past the gravitational pull of yearning, avoiding, distraction, and conceptualization — veil after veil — until a type of mental zero gravity was achieved. My mind was extremely fluid and buoyant at this stage, as I began to observe the most fundamental level of mind, the fabric of consciousness itself. It was seen as rapidly arising and vanishing mind units of experience. I witnessed that who I am is nothing more than a quickly arising and disappearing moment-to-moment sequence of mental and physical phenomena. There was no permanent self within it all; even the observer of all this was recognized as arising and passing away with each moment. Ultimately, no one was home, so it seemed.

At the same time I could see that these separate, yet interrelated moments of experience were the canvas on which our individual personalities, memories, hopes, and dreams are holographically imprinted. The psychological and conceptual realm was illusory, ephemeral, and endless from this vantage point — like a hologram, empty and real at the same time. Real in that it exists, and empty in that it is empty of self. The idea of self was just that, an *idea* that had no tangible existence, any more than there is an equator one can touch circumscribing the earth. Self, like the equator, exists only as ideas in consciousness and has no objective reality other than *thought.* Here again the Buddha's comment made sense: "The path there is, but no one who walks it; deeds are done, but no one who does them; suffering exists, but no one who suffers; nirvana is, but no one who enters it."

Hence the weeks drifted into months, with a clear noticing of mental and physical phenomena simply arising and passing away in the cognitive sea of consciousness. As the awareness of changing objects matured, the sittings became subtler, more nuanced. As they did, I noticed, once again, how easy it would be to merge with this oceanic state of transparent stillness. But upon more intimate discernment, it, too, wasn't stationary. It, too, was propped up by conditions. It, too, was inherently insubstantial. It could not be trusted.

Even the mind that was aware of this understanding was changing. No matter what state arose within consciousness, there was an awareness that *knew* there was no place to rest or seek asylum. As this insight matured all states took on the feel of a seductive spiritual trap. Rapture and luminosity were empty of centrality. Insight too was without ownership. Consciousness was a house of ephemeral cards. It seemed to me at this stage of meditation that nothing was ultimately worth diving into and saying, "Yes, this is it! Dharma pay dirt." Every condition was a condition — a potential snare. Therefore every condition was innately laced with suffering — *dukkha.* Gross or subtle suffering, it didn't matter. Conditionality itself was suffering, or so I thought at the time. Thus, my mind — or I should say "the conditional constituents of liberation," as U Pandita called it — began to seriously incline toward a deeply internal sense of a nonoccurrence of consciousness.

In nearly imperceptible degrees of intuitive realizations, insight informed the mind that even the most sublime states of consciousness were insubstantial and conditioned. At the same time I knew on a gut level just how precarious it all was. At any moment, anything could happen and the mind would lose this quality of heightened presence, and in a flash, you would return to the former bandwidth, where resisting and craving this or that felt normal, even desirable. Although I had had the insight before, this time the knowledge sent a chill up my spine. It translated into one thing: I wanted to know existential authenticity, a radical transcendence of the known. If knowing was suffering — then I wanted to know a supramundane knowing that was beyond all known conditions, beyond time — nirvana.

Throughout this period Sayadaw U Pandita's instructions were complex and detailed. While providing this guidance, he continued to demonstrate a warm and composed simplicity. Both direct and unenthusiastic, he communicated that there was nothing to get excited about nor anything special to anticipate. He would say, "Rest in the truth that it is awareness that liberates the mind from ignorance not one's desire for freedom."

At another session he told me, "Let conditions liberate conditions. In other words, let Dharma processes liberate Dharma processes." In addition, he said, "There is nothing *you* need to do. When the Dharma needs to liberate itself, it will."

I took his words to heart. In so doing, it was amazing to watch awareness completely dissolve the sense of *doer* in meditation. U Pandita would say, "Now you understand meditation without meditator. Knowing without a knower. Just mental and physical processes arising and disappearing in a naturally occurring mystery that we don't know the why for." I took this to mean that consciousness was now in synchronicity with itself.

I was amazed to see how meditation naturally disabused consciousness of its insidious tendency to fixate, fuse, grasp, or glom onto some phenomenon — a sensation, an emotion, an insight — as "my" experience, "my" feeling, "my" understanding. This unquestioned habit to selectively fixate with certain interior images and ideas revealed that in the absence of fixation there was also the absence of conflict. For Sayadaw U Pandita and the classical teachings of the Buddha, the endgame was an insight that shattered core ignorance so fully that fixation was permanently dissolved, and therefore core conflict ceased, permanently. Anything less, U Pandita told me, "was a partial realization."

As I further relaxed the fixation to my ideas of myself as "me," I occupied more of myself. Self-identification was myopic. The absence of self-fixation was fullness. Consciousness was manifesting in its most natural expression. It was amazing to see that mind, through intensive meditation — the practice of sustained awareness — could be programmed to intimately enter and observe itself, to understand and liberate its own functionings. I realized that I no longer had to become free. Rather, a natural process of liberation had been activated. The Dharma was simply observing, feeling, intuiting, knowing its own most primal machinations. Within it was the transparent wisdom of pure being — at times free, at times lucid, at times tired, then awake again in wonderment, and so on throughout the day. There was no time or location in this process. In a referenceless universe, without an absolute up or down, past or future, forward or backward, I deeply understood that there is only a natural simultaneity. What else to call the "everywhere-at-once-ness" of the cosmos that was arising through the prism of my limited consciousness?

From this vantage point, the mind seemed to stop moving toward or away from anything. Where could you go in a universe that never began nor will ever end? This realization took me beyond any need or strategy whatsoever. Nothing to accept nor reject. *Life is what it is* — nothing more, nothing less, full and empty at the same time.

When I went to see Mahasi Sayadaw for my weekly session, he called this realization "a glimpse of suchness," or in the Pali Buddhist language, he said, "we call this *sunnata.* It's normal. It, too, is subject to change. There are much more compelling realms of Dharma understanding and liberation. Neither long for this state to continue nor hope for something deeper to arise in the future."

He went on to explain how the Buddha had described the liberated mind to be like a diamond. "The diamond mind," he said, "was a mind that understood the nature of suffering — all things change and are inherently without self-reference. The diamond mind also knows the origin of suffering — one knows that yearning and avoiding lead to grasping and fixation. The diamond mind also knows the cessation of suffering — the unconditioned freedom of nirvana — that place beyond time. And the diamond mind knows without a doubt the requisites of consciousness that progressively lead to the liberation from suffering — awareness of the mind, right now.

"When awareness becomes mature, unremitting wisdom will dispel the most transparent veils of ignorance. Then the liberated mind will appear, luminous, radiant, and free. We call this the diamond mind."

Over the course of the next few months the quality of awareness became even suppler. The meditations became an effortless flow of transparent wakefulness. Nearly imperceptible forms of wanting and avoiding vanished. As self-fixation was further freed, friction relaxed. As the mind became less weighty, inner gravity had less of a hold, and as such there was an upsurge of scintillating joy. Every molecule of consciousness felt like it was being fondled with inexplicable subtlety. At times I laughed and cried simultaneously. It was the most sublime satisfaction I had ever known.

Among the more interesting aspects of the intensive meditation process at this point was to see how the mind transcended all need in faith, beliefs, outcomes, attitudes, and identities. "The human" was a psychical process, inherently empty of centrality. With mature mindfulness the mind observes itself effortlessly and as a result, consciousness discovers the substructures of its own being. From an understanding of impermanence — *anicca* — the mind progressively released clinging. From an understanding of suchness — *anatta* — the mind dissolved ignorance, the belief in a permanent, separate self. From an understanding of conditioned arising — *dukkha* — consciousness abided in its natural state, a transparent cognitive weightlessness.

Generally, whenever I noticed even a whisper of anticipation for "an enlightened outcome" to a sitting, I reflected on just one line from the Buddha: "Nirvana is, but no one enters it." This helped me to relax the "I" out of the suchness and be without the "me."

The last stage was when the physical body itself began to disappear. Form was gone for long periods of time. This left just consciousness aware of itself, until it too disappeared. For several moments consciousness stopped arising. There was the cessation of knowing — the absence of presence — the zero point beyond being. I stayed at this stage for a few weeks.

When I went to Mahasi Sayadaw to discuss my practice, at the end of the session he read from one of his books the following passage attributed to the Buddha: "The nirvana to which one's mind is inclined is real. But it has no elements of earth, water, fire, and air. It is neither the realm of infinity of space. Nor the realm of infinity of consciousness. Nor the realm of nothingness. Nor the realm of neither perception nor not perception. It denotes neither this world nor other worlds. No moon nor sun shines there. I never maintain that in nirvana there are goings and comings. It has no foothold or residence. It is Deathless, Unborn, and Unformed. It has no abode. Nothing ever occurs there. It has no sense-objects. It is the end of suffering."

THE END OF THE BEGINNING

Days later, in August 1982, as I was discussing with U Pandita my meditation experience, which had now shifted from *vipassana* to *metta* meditation — the practice of loving-kindness — Mahasi Sayadaw's attendant rushed into the cottage and told us that Mahasi just collapsed at his desk and was unconscious. Sayadaw U Pandita and I raced to Mahasi's residence a few doors down. In a few minutes the ambulance arrived and took him to Rangoon General Hospital, where he was diagnosed as having had a massive stroke. Mahasi never regained consciousness and died two days later.

Over the next week, as his body lay in state, it was easy to see the impact this great man had on the lives of so many people. Braving torrential monsoon rains, several hundred thousand people, sometimes four abreast and a mile long, poured into the monastery from all over the country and around the world to pay their final respects to one of the greatest meditation masters of our era.

I'll never forget the day his body was burned. At the site of the cremation over a hundred thousand people stood as Sayadaw U Pandita took the microphone and led the gathering in a short Pali chant. I think he quoted the final words of the Buddha, spoken just before his death. "All conditioned things in this world are impermanent. To understand this law is the highest happiness. Strive on friends, with diligence." I felt no sadness at this time, only gratitude. This man's life was a legendary example of harmlessness, compassion, and wisdom. His teachings on insight meditation have spread worldwide.

Mahasi Sayadaw provided me with the ground on which my life sits today. Without intensive meditation I would have little understanding of the complex world in my mind and heart. I will be forever honored to have been his first long-term American Dharma student, as well as that of Sayadaw U Pandita. And although much of my Dharma understanding has expanded from my time in the monastery, the basis of what I share in my retreats today, "World Dharma, natural freedom, and undifferentiated awareness meditation," contains their insights, and doesn't reject a thing.

Days after Mahasi Sayadaw's passing, I was told by the authorities once again to leave the country. Soon thereafter I chose to disrobe as a monk and face my life in the world. My life as a monk had come to an end. I had no idea at the time of the people's "revolution of the spirit" that had been brewing during those years in the monastery. Little did I know that my next twenty years of involvement with Burma would be incomparably more complex and compelling than any insight gained in meditation.

In some mysterious yet real way, I feel that my Dharma life began on the day I disrobed as a monk. This was the end of the beginning.

◆ POLITICIZED PRESENCE — LIFE BEYOND NIRVANA

The director of the monastery bought me a ticket to Bangkok. From there I made my way south to the island where it all started years before. My return to Ko Samui Island in the South China Sea opened my eyes to a world I had never seen. It began one day when, on an isolated stretch of beach, I noticed five men walking toward the shoreline. I could see three large objects lying on the sand in front of them. When I got closer I saw they were three mutilated bodies — bloated, decomposing masses of black, red, and blue. The stench that hung in the still morning air was more alarming than the wretchedness of death itself. Flies were swarming in huge clusters, buzzing and sucking from open gashes.

"I'm Hans, Interpol," the tall blond declared. Next to him stood four Thai police, expressionless.

"What happened?" I asked. "Who are they?"

"Vietnamese. Boat people. We found three hundred of them the past few days. This is nothing new. We see it all the time."

Overhead a flock of frenzied gulls cried. I'd seen dead bodies before but nothing like this. I couldn't tell if they were men or women. The bodies were too mutilated to know. Large chunks of flesh were missing. Eyes were missing. Arms had been chopped off. There were large gashes through their skulls, chests, and thighs.

"That one," Hans said pointing toward what was probably a

woman. "Look . . . the bastards slit her throat. And that gash between her legs . . . probably yanked her baby right out of her. Some of these Thai pirates are subhuman."

I stood in silence, fighting to get beyond my horror.

Hans continued in a monotone. "It's difficult for us to know the real story of what happens out there. Few ever live to tell. Maybe forty, fifty, sometimes sixty or more refugees are on these boats. They are without weapons, most are near death from exposure and starvation. They drift for weeks, sometimes months. They risk their lives for the remote chance of a better life across the sea.

"The pirates zoom in with high-powered motorboats. They're hungry for the gold and gems the refugees have with them. The refugees who jump overboard are shot while floundering in the sea. Others have their hands and feet cut off, then they're thrown overboard. Those left on deck are bludgeoned to death with clubs, hatchets, and machetes.

"The attractive women, after being gang-raped, are often kept as sex slaves or sold as prostitutes to brothels in Bangkok. No one is spared before the boat is set on fire or sunk with machine-gun fire."

Hans walked away.

After the bodies were photographed, local fishermen sacked the remains and carried them over their backs to a waiting truck. As I walked on I noticed how the gulls swooped down for the few pieces of flesh that remained. I remember kicking the sand and wondering how you can find joy in life, knowing this kind of insanity is all around.

I reflected on the quality of human conscience — the ability to discern right from wrong — and its role in the Dharma. Conscience is intimately tied to integrity, decency, and dignity — the pillars of a civilized life. Conscience is our inner compass — an intuitive intelligence that respects life and creates goodness and liberty.

It is my belief that conscience is the soul of consciousness and the wisdom of liberation. But empowering conscience as a guide in life is complex. In the monastery I had the opportunity to focus exclusively on me, and pretty much me alone, until I was awakened from my self-fixation by illness and by the example of others who came to me to show me another way of being. Self-fixation seems to dull or distort conscience to serve one's self-interest. At other times self-fixation makes conscience nearly inaudible and replaces it with the loud voice of cynicism, narcissism, or hopelessness.

Excuses for not listening to conscience are innumerable. Even when we hear and feel conscience, it is often split between two good reasons to do or not to do, competing for action or inaction. This presents a dilemma. Should I or shouldn't I? To be or to act? To give or withdraw? To speak out or stay quiet? To join the revolution or stay on the couch? Pursue my freedom or serve others' freedom, or both?

Or, I often hear in retreats and lectures the question of who's making the choice anyway? Is it God's will or my will? Am i or Am I? Are we driving the car, or are we being dragged by forces beyond our control? How much reality can I create and how much destiny must I eat? How much of life is free and how much is fate? How much of the spiritual life is biologically conditioned and how much freedom is actually ours to choose? There are numerous ways to ask how much choice we ever have.

Life is a moment-to-moment process of decisions. And the thin line between right and wrong choices — between the life I'm leading and the life I could be leading — is often a hair's breadth in difference.

Victor Frankl, the Viennese psychiatrist, from his years in

Auschwitz, made this observation: "We who lived in concentration camps can remember those who walked through the huts comforting others, giving away their last piece of bread. They may have been few in number, but they offer sufficient proof that everything can be taken from a person but one thing: the last of human freedoms — to choose one's attitude in any given set of circumstances — to choose one's own way."

◆ LOOKING BACK, THEN AND NOW

The first phase of my Dharma life was primarily motivated by one thing: my needs — my need to be free, my need to awaken, my need to realize nirvana, my need to escape suffering, my need to know myself by me looking in the mirror of me looking back at me. Since Buddhism and much of Eastern mysticism are rooted in the belief that the individual creates his and her own suffering, seeking "the truth of me" made a lot of sense at the time.

I further authenticated my style of seeking by holding fast to a worldview that invalidated the outer world as having any value to inner awakening, other than a reminder of what a samsaric nightmare it was out there. It was seen as unwise to build a life on the quicksand of time. Based on that dogma, I sought refuge inside, searching for that special nirvanic real estate that time could not touch.

According to Eastern-oriented spirituality, the external world, *samsara,* is not only inherently unsatisfactory but a self-generated illusion. The outer world exists only as the projection of one's ignorance, dreaming the world of name and form into existence. This philosophical vantage point throws material existence into question. Life as it usually appears is empty of inherent reality: trees do not exist, people do not exist, babies are not born, the sun does not shine, wars are not fought. Time, gender, nations, race, borders — the cosmos itself — do not exist, except as self-generated phantoms projected onto the sky of one's mind. Empty phenomena alone exist, but apart from this limitless submolecular quantum wilderness, there is nothing except having an enlightened perspective about it. An enlightened perspective, that is, without an ultimate self that is experiencing enlightenment.

As the supposition goes, you can travel the world seeking truth, or meditate for decades on end, but unless you divest yourself of fusion with conceptualization and wake up from the primordial trance, you will remain in the hallucination of your own delusions, much like an actor who keeps acting once the show is over, somehow forgetting his or her real-life identity or true nature.

I believed the theory. I accepted that I couldn't walk out of my own movie. I also affirmed that I did not want to rescript a new story, nor play a new, more compelling character. If every expression of "me," every self and subself, was in fact a self-generated illusion, why choose a ghostlike existence when I could have a real one? After all, the Buddha had made it clear that 100 percent of one's suffering came from self-fixation. That meant that 100 percent of one's freedom came from relaxing fixation to self and all subselves. In other words, the best self in Buddhism is no-self. Even being an authentic self is missing the point. The only true story is "no story" and therefore one must dissolve into the one and only freedom — the ultimate nonstory — that of union with emptiness, or zeroness, or nirvana — the unconditioned vacuum of transpersonal suchness. Accepting all that I am — a fleshy, lusty, emotional, complex, vibrant self, consisting of many dimensions and identities — definitely does not fit the bill in this narrative.

As the theory goes, freeing the mind of one's primordial ignorance is considered a great act of compassion. I wanted to do both myself and the world a service by liberating myself from the gravitational pull of fear, anger, lust, and all other forms of self-centered fixation. In order to accomplish this spiritual duty, as I saw it, I needed very specific assistance. The Buddha was emphatic that overcoming self-grasping was "more difficult than conquering a thousand enemy soldiers single-handedly a thousand different times" — almost impossible.

In retrospect I see how the meditation guides I trained with in Burma were shamanistic. Many of the traditional South American shamans and their Western counterparts use entheogenic substances, which often take one out of body into radical frontiers of hyperdimensional interior space. My meditative guides encouraged exploration of consciousness through the organic substances of awareness, energy, and extreme focus.

The meditation center became a launchpad — a mission control for consciousness. Everything we did was directed toward internal zero gravity: direct experience of a mind free of any interest whatsoever in identifying with concepts, people, things, or preferences. Thoughts are the gravity that keeps you earth-bound. My guides supported me in transcending every desire to ever want to participate in ordinary human existence again.

Desire is the greatest obstacle to Eastern-oriented forms of liberation. In his Second Noble Truth, the Buddha identified desire as the root of suffering. Desire is pathologized as a friction in the mind rooted in the belief in a "self" who wants something. Because mental frictions inhibit inner weightlessness, the only way into this existential float zone is to suspend and sustain the absolute absence of desire.

Classical transpersonal Eastern spirituality, Buddhism included, believes that desire keeps the human imprisoned and desirelessness is the only true freedom. Anything less than the absolute absence of desire is considered mental gravity, the opposite of the *en-light-en-ing* process of consciousness. The idea of becoming a well-integrated, whole human being fully functioning in the world is not part of this equation.

As every entheogenic psychonaught can tell you, achieving transpersonal states of consciousness presents its own dilemmas. As alluring as they can be, the reentry into personal life can be maddening. Integrating these states within one's body, within form, as a sexual being living in the world — creating, working, communicating — can be, and almost always is, disorienting. Almost every astronaut who goes into space and experiences weightlessness, upon coming back to earth, back into gravity, says how depressing it is. Besides having a body that suddenly feels much heavier, reentering the gridlock of daily life isn't an easy adjustment.

This begs the question: Does one even need to become an astronaut in order to become a better human here on earth? Does one even need to experience emotional zero gravity, setting aside all the cosmological myths associated with the experience, to appreciate one's body, open one's lungs to breathe more deeply, to relate to the people around us, or feel the preciousness of every day of one's life? Does one need an out-of-body experience to understand freedom or the limitations of fear? And is desire a force that can only be controlled through renunciation, through refusal?

Although practicing desirelessness may be well suited to a life in a monastery, it isn't necessarily the best game plan out here in the world. No matter how far you go, out or in, sooner or later you come back to earth, to the body, to desires, to fears, to your humanness.

Desirelessness, or any other state of "absence from," is what

Isaiah Berlin described as negative freedom. To subdue the mind in an attempt to extinguish desire is a dominator metaphor, a "conquest of," rather than an "alchemy into." Although negative forms of freedom are important, they seem best accomplished through positive liberty — the freedom to creatively develop and realize a greater good. Positive freedom means embracing the whole of one's being, not as an ideal but as an experience of expansion, inclusion, and dimension. This includes ambiguity and uncertainty. It includes reality — material reality and desire. Let us not forget that we are embodied beings — lusty, breathing, raw, fragile, aging, pulsing, caring, frightened, wanting.

I believe that Buddhism's great contribution to society is its brilliant analysis of consciousness and meditation — the transformational power of sustained awareness. In fact, I think Buddhism should be awarded the Nobel Peace Prize for bringing awareness-based intensive meditation into the world. As a means to explore enhanced states of consciousness it is unsurpassed. But the Buddhist belief system that frames the meditative exploration of consciousness also has its limits. As a religion, as a doctrine in its whole, Buddhism and much of Eastern mysticism espouse a paradigm of absolute certainty about a universe of infinite mystery. And that doesn't square with me. It is impossible to have absolute truths coming from the biologically dependent, mythmaking mammals that we are — just a few aeons up from our single-cell sea ancestors! Every culture concocts its own creation fables and cosmic laws and enshrines them on the cave walls of its consciousness. Buddhism is only one out of more than three hundred other world religions, and no one of them has the ultimate scoop on the grand scheme. I had never seriously questioned these issues during my years as a monk, or afterward, when I taught in the West.

Clearly, we must learn to live with cosmic ambiguity while struggling for greater truths. Pierre Teilhard de Chardin informs us of both the struggle and its resolution: "When every certainty is shaken and every utterance fails, when every principle seems doubtful, then there is one ultimate belief that can guide our inner life: the belief in an absolute direction of growth to which our duty and our happiness demands we should conform."

EVOLVING REALISTIC ATTITUDE

The Dharma life, that of following our instinct for freedom, requires involvement in everything. Every emotion, every mind state, every expression of being is valuable, important to know and learn from. Evolving a realistic Dharma attitude helps to keep these things in perspective.

At times the process is arduous and all-consuming, requiring heroic patience, courage, and determination. At other times, the way is silent, intuitive, and imperceptible. It can be a magical process, whereby we smile as we absorb life's delicious blend of beauty and intrigue. Then, without notice, a storm of torment, origin unknown, sweeps over us and takes us to our knees. Being alive and engaged with all dimensions of reality is an odyssey no one can prepare us for. No amount of training or spiritual practice makes direct experience any less daunting. By embracing freedom as our most treasured quality, we empower an uninhibited exploration of the mysterious realms of human consciousness; we integrate these discoveries, come what may, into all the domains of our life.

With discernment and intelligence as our guides, we'll be required to enter the fiery mouth of many strange and terrifying circumstances. Life is simply too vast and unpredictable to assume that the unthinkable will not occur. As realists we stay alert and ready to enter sadness, loneliness, and even terror. We may expect to be thrust into the darkest abyss, where hopelessness and depression overwhelm our value of life and our motivation to continue the work of liberation. Sometimes it may bring us to the edge of madness.

Realistic spiritual discovery is an involvement in everything we hoped to avoid. I'm not suggesting that you defensively brace yourself for the crisis to come, or even anticipate torment and pain, but the heart will not genuinely open until all of life's realities are admitted. Loss and grieving are not only natural but divinely honorable. If you risk loving life and others, you will inevitably confront the truth that all things must pass.

Fostering realistic Dharma attitude helps to counterbalance the forces of spiritual grandiosity, idealism, and false expectations. Each of us must learn the consequences of our actions. Transformational insight, psychological harmony, and unbound freedom are compelling goals. Rather than thwart these beautiful impulses or temper our enthusiasm for these noble aims, we should appreciate them as points of light in a vision, and skillfully use goals to release ourselves into the open space of natural freedom. We must be both relaxed and attentive, able to rest and play at the same time. We must strive to sustain a vital hope and an even peace in each moment. To name and strive for personal goals while keeping a mind free of conclusions is a stunning accomplishment, one that must be attempted over and over again.

Equally, it is important to disabuse ourselves of unreasonable spiritual ideals and developmental expectations. The Dharma life is not free of conflict. To hope that your spiritual work will rid you of all unwanted problems or eliminate internal disharmony is an alluring but erroneous goal. Rather than gliding smoothly along, you are likely to struggle, curse, and cry your way down the road of freedom along with the rest of us. No matter how sincere and profound, you will continue to experience periods of suffering until you die. No one is beyond it. No one has completely rid themselves of the inherent tensions and conflicts within the psyche. No one is abiding in an absolute state of perfect psychological harmony. No one has removed the tormenting emotions of greed, anger, and delusion. The ocean of consciousness is simply too vast and too complex to fully explore and wisely understand during the brevity of a single lifetime.

Perhaps the full mapping of consciousness and the cosmos will never be achieved. Perhaps it's not even necessary. Living with existential uncertainty can be wonderful. With realistic Dharma attitude we are more concerned with declaring our willingness to face situations openly and learn what we can in the most basic, human ways.

Being human is a destiny fraught with every conceivable obstacle. We realize progressive liberation as we begin to allow ourselves to feel the terrible burden of our honest inner life. By acknowledging inner claustrophobia, we act to expand our space. Realistic Dharma attitude is an ongoing vow to willfully align ourselves to freedom, refusing to be held in the safety of the familiar or the comfortable. It requires courage to challenge the bondage and addiction to frictionless lifestyles and narcissism. We must see the difference between the "ease of being" and the "struggle for excellence."

Following the instinct for freedom requires knowing that there is no wrong time to learn. At moments the Dharma life will feel like an exotic adjunct to our life. At other times it will seem that there is nothing separate from the process. It's a journey of experience that begins and ends right now — everywhere, always.

Fundamentally, the language of the Dharma is not found through the intellect; it's transconceptual. This requires feeling your way into reality. The Dharma is an intuitive opening and often clumsy and erratic. It is not precise or mathematical. We are called upon to walk the thin line of accepting our imperfect humanness without compromising our ideals and goals. It means always walking into the future knowing that birth and death are present. It is a journey inward and outward, simultaneously. Each moment contains the forwards and the backwards. We are called to live in the sacred space of being full and broken at the same time.

To learn and honor our inherent interconnectedness may be the most challenging task before us. This, the World Dharma of shared presence, forms the basis of the final section of the book.

PART THREE

WORLD DHARMA — LIBERATION THROUGH LIVING

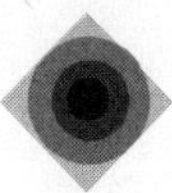

THE MYSTERIOUS TOTALITY THAT WE ARE

Outer life — as seen through the senses and the circuitry of consciousness — is a hyperspatial vibrancy of complex energy patterns. A human face is one such pattern, as is making love. But whose face is it, and who's making love with whom? Physicists tell us that beneath visual life, beneath how we ordinarily perceive things, lies a shimmering sea of subatomic particles, and humans are holographic excitations consisting of those very same particles. Universal intelligence may be so multidimensional that life as we know it — every aspect of the cosmos — may be the inside of a single molecule of DNA. We may be a molecule of God among hundreds of trillions of other God molecules within a being — an entity, a person, a form of life — we have no idea about. Or maybe we are so microscopic that our infinity is a single cell in the cerebral cortex of a creature crawling along a corridor somewhere in some world — a creature imprinted with the memory of the evolutionary code of consciousness, while oblivious to the greater context of its life, the infinite cosmos. It's possible. That's life — an unfathomable sea of potentialities: a magnificent and maddening blend of organic intelligence that bleeds, weeps, and makes love with itself. Thus, we know ourselves to be — conscious life. It's no wonder humankind concocts creation myths and spins spiritual strategies in order to try to make some sense of it all, to bring it under control. We are in an awesome situation.

Whatever life is, we are a microcosm of a mysterious totality. We are paradoxically bound within a membrane that allows for our own uniqueness while also being inseparable from the whole. The confluence of opposite, yet simultaneous, worlds — that of self with other, mortality with eternity, spirit with matter, life with death, ignorance with wisdom, creativity with determinism, certainty with ambiguity, and liberation with bondage — creates in us a yearning for some kind of reconciliation that is forever out of reach.

Life is a polarity of opposites, a simultaneous heaven and hell, a yin yang of torture and ecstasy, not easily reconciled this or that way. It is our instinct for freedom that compels us to push the boundaries of our confinement, seeking to transform chaos and confusion with intuition and reason, dancing at the edge, where knowledge and love emerge from mystery.

On my final day in Burma back in 1996 I met with U Kyi Maung, my eighty-year-old Burmese friend and mentor. As a freedom fighter within Burma's nonviolent revolution, he has been imprisoned twice, spending eleven years in solitary confinement. I feared he would be rearrested at any moment. Soldiers loyal to the dictatorship were on the road outside the compound. I asked him, "Sir, if you are rearrested, what words would you like to leave for others to carry on the struggle for freedom."

In a slow and reflective tone he replied, "For the coming generations I would emphasize two most important things: education and a deep sense of history. Knowledge is essential. They should learn about the world at large. This will assist them in shaping their own lives, freely.

"To grasp history is to grasp the importance of interrelatedness — the causes, conditions, and consequences of thought and action and how they affect the development or demise of civilization — human existence at large. Everyone plays a part. The gift of life is to play that part with profound responsibility. The twentieth century has taught us great lessons in all aspects of human involvement. There have been some advances humankind could never have imagined. In this century we have seen the folly of ideologies, such as Fascism and State Communism, which are inconsistent with creativity and the flourishing of the spirit. From the nineteenth century came the rise of the British Empire that sent a plague of exploitation around the world. Yet it too was humbled. We have witnessed all types of conflict, from urban violence to global wars, from bolt-action rifles to the nuclear bomb, typewriters to computers, a revolution in music and dance. There's just so much, and within it all have come a few good men and women with vision, that remarkable gift to see our tomorrow today. Their gifts are renewing our hopes for the future of the planet, and our survival as a species. It's all about interrelatedness. From its full exploration I believe will come the flourishing of civilization, and not its untimely demise."

He paused briefly. "As for me, don't worry. What I care about the most, and practice off and on throughout the day, is to be aware. That's all. To be aware. See, I have pieces of paper in my pockets that I carry with me: quotes, inspiring reminders. They refocus my mind on the here and now. That is the most important thing to me. To be present. Awake. Aware. My eleven years in prison were severe, but I used the time to my advantage. I never forget that what I am seeing now — that pale green line streaking across the pond, or the shadow of the tree across your leg — disappears the moment I turn my face. This is life's simplicity. Just the here and now. Aware that nothing is permanent.

"That barbed-wire fence across the back of Aung San Suu Kyi's compound over there — why worry about the presence of such an irritant? It's insignificant. Now if I worry about anything, it's that I might lose this sense of awareness. So I guard it as something precious. Things pass . . . that I have seen. Life is what you make it, now. So let us put our energies into life. Into understanding our interrelatedness. In this way I try not to lose my perspective."

I spent six months meeting with this wise statesman. I had bonded deeply with all he stood for, with Burma's struggle for freedom, and how their struggle "over there" is connected with our struggle for freedom "right here."

With characteristic warmth U Kyi Maung said, "Don't worry. When death comes, let it come. What I do fear, however, is that I would be so weak that I would choose the easiest way out, to lie around in bed all day and read some book on the collapse of yet another totalitarian regime." I had a tear in my eye as he walked me to the door and said good-bye.

MY RELATIONSHIPS ARE ME

I started this book with a basic recognition: life experience is our greatest teacher and therefore our genuine source for spiritual awakening. It is awareness that liberates, not a teacher, nor a doctrine, nor a form. I would like to extend that essential understanding by saying life experience is *lived experience.* We don't just sit by the side of the river and watch it go by. The point is to immerse oneself in it. In reality, there is no place one can stand to be outside of life looking in at it, no matter how we might try. We are life. Life is us. In this way the World Dharma view transcends all dichotomies between mind and matter, self and world, the individual and relationship. I am my relationships. My relationships are me. We are alive within a whole universe of interrelated life. By feeling the *living reality* of mutual being we become radically alive to the ever-present magic of learning from each other, and growing together. We feel both our individuality and our unity at the confluence of where the inner meets the outer. This awareness is a simultaneous presence of belonging that transcends observer and observed, subject and object, inner and outer, self and other, personal and transpersonal, spirit and world.

When I have entered this space of belonging I have learned the greatest lessons in life. It is where I have touched, broken open, celebrated, rejected, burned, awakened, been hurt, cried, fallen in love, and created. When I entered relatedness, rather than avoiding relationship, it has brought me closer to others, to life, and myself, together as one. It has been the way to understand the words of Jesus when he said, "When you make the two one, and when you make the inner as the outer and the outer as the inner, and the above as the below, and when you make the male and female into a single one — then shall you enter the Kingdom." To me that's World Dharma — a liberating communion with simultaneity.

World Dharma is the wisdom of shared presence and co-creative evolution. It sees no ultimate separation, no duality, no demarcation where self and other begin or end. When in doubt, I ask myself if I am avoiding relationship or engaging it. This Dharma is not about being here now with myself alone, but being here now, together, so we grow. World Dharma points to what Julian Huxley so brilliantly described: "man discovers that he is nothing else than evolution become conscious of itself." And this evolution is happening to us all, simultaneously.

◆ EXISTENTIAL HUMANNESS

But what is the driving beat of World Dharma, the wisdom that compels you to get up and dance? The question takes me back to Burma for the answer — to a time just a few days before I disrobed as a monk. It had been arranged by elders at my monastery that I be given an audience with Tipitakadara Sayadaw — Burma's most respected monk and most recognized bodhisattva. Bodhisattva in the Theravada Buddhist tradition refers to someone who has promised to find his or her own liberation through serving the liberation of others.

In Burma, a country with five thousand monasteries and more than one million monks and nuns, the eighty-year-old Tipitakadara Sayadaw was the most renowned authority on the Buddha's teachings. Before my meeting with the Sayadaw, elders explained to me how the Buddha's teachings had been preserved over the past twenty-six centuries, and the contribution that Tipitakadara Sayadaw had made in modern times. They said that the teachings were brought forward by six Great Buddhist Councils. The first four councils took place in India, one hundred years apart, after the Buddha's death. Two millennia later, in 1868, the Fifth Council took place in the city of Mandalay, in upcountry Burma. The Sixth Council, in 1954, was organized by the first prime minster of Burma and was held in Rangoon. The last council brought together several thousand prominent monks, nuns, and lay practitioners from the five main Theravada

Buddhist countries of Burma, Thailand, Cambodia, Laos, and Sri Lanka.

Each of the six councils brought together members of the Buddhist clergy — the *sangha* — for two key purposes: to determine the actual teachings of the Buddha and to agree on their most salient meaning. At each of the six councils two main *sangha* members were appointed by the synod to conduct the proceedings. One monk was designated to recite the teachings and served to answer questions posed by the chief interrogator, the second most important person at the council.

The role of the congregation was to scrutinize the Dharma dialogue between the chief interrogator and chief answerer. When the congregation was satisfied with the wisdom of the exchange, and the chief questioner and answerer both agreed, there would be a final confirmation about both the letter and meaning of the particular teaching being examined.

In this way the six councils went through the three groupings of the traditional teachings: the discourses of the Buddha, the teachings on existential psychology, and the rules of conduct for the *sangha*. When all three aspects of the traditional Dharma had been discussed and agreement was reached, the council concluded and the teachings were said to be "accurate" and "reestablished."

The Sixth Council had appointed my main teacher, Mahasi Sayadaw, as the chief interrogator and Tipitakadara Sayadaw as the chief answerer. For the three years the Sixth Council convened, Mahasi Sayadaw asked Tipitakadara Sayadaw the most complex questions about the salient meaning of the Dharma according to the Buddha's teachings. And for three years, several thousand monks and nuns from every Theravada Buddhist country listened to the dialogue between the two senior *sangha* members. This dialogue represented the essence of the fifty-two traditional Pali Buddhist texts and their established commentaries, totalling approximately ten thousand pages.

Keeping this in mind, when I was given an audience with Tipitakadara Sayadaw, I asked this first question: "What, Sir, is the living essence of the Buddha's teachings? If I never read a Buddhist book, never read a page of the classical texts, what is the only thing I need to know to understand those teachings? What is the only thing necessary to know about those teachings in order to find liberation through living in this very life?"

As I asked the question he listened with a calm intensity, looking at me through his large black glasses with an unflinching gaze. He then leaned forward and said in a slow, even tone, "Know what you do." As he let his words fill the silence he held my eyes with his own, then continued to speak. "To *know* yourself. That is the essence."

That's it, I thought, ten thousand pages and twenty-six centuries later, four words, "know what you do," and another three, "to know yourself." That's the essence?

Over the next two hours we had a dialogue that went straight to my heart. Although I didn't really get the impact of it at the time, it was one of those spiritual teachings that would progressively flower over the following decades to become embodied in the practical application of World Dharma.

This elder monk offered a perspective on the Dharma life I would call existential humanness, a liberating transpersonal wisdom born from engaging human interrelatedness — with self, with others, and with the world.

AWAKENED PRESENCE — A LIBERATING INTIMACY

The elder Sayadaw went on to explain what he meant by the phrase "to know." On the most basic level "to know" was to clearly comprehend what was actually happening within yourself as it occurred. It wasn't a delayed presence, but a radical immediacy. "If you are thinking," he said, "know yourself to be thinking. If you are walking, know that you are walking. If you are feeling love, know that you are feeling love.

"As you are sitting on the floor right now," he continued, "know yourself as such." The most essential nature of the mind is to know, to comprehend, to cognize. The nature of consciousness is easily influenced with a variety of mind qualities. These qualities modify the otherwise transparent nature of consciousness. When you are restless, for example, this mind quality is like a strong wind blowing across the ocean of consciousness, creating a choppy surface. When the mind is calm, the surface becomes still. But to occupy the Dharma is to *know* them and *know that you are knowing* them. "The knowing should remain," Tipitakadara Sayadaw told me. I came to understand them as the trio of the sun, clouds, and sunlight. The sun is consciousness, clouds are mind states, and the sunlight is the *knowing.*

As he continued I sensed that he was skillfully guiding me into a shared state of "awakened presence" — a simultaneity of us, sitting together in a room, awake.

I asked him, "Sir, what then is the essence of this *knowing?*"

He replied, "The essence of knowing is to understand the practical application of these three Pali Buddhist words: *dana, sila,* and *bhavana.* It is from knowing these three qualities that *knowing,* or Dharma understanding, matures."

Dana is the quality of giving, but he emphasized that *dana* is a multidimensional quality that exceeds mere generosity alone. It is a way of being, open and available — conscientious of sharing time, energy, and material things, as well as creating opportunities for others. *Sila* is the quality of ethical integrity. It is rooted in harmlessness and functions to harmonize the liberating aspects of consciousness. He stressed that a mind rooted in *sila* is essentially incorruptible, that *sila* and dignity go hand in hand.

Bhavana is the process by which the Dharma beautifies consciousness, he concluded. At the time I knew the word *bhavana* only in the context of intensive silent meditation practice, so I asked him to please explain the deeper meaning of the concept. He seemed a bit surprised that I wasn't fluent with the word since the original name of my teacher — Mahasi Sayadaw — was Sayadaw U Sobhana. The Pali word *sobhana* pointed to the beautiful qualities of consciousness, or the factors of mind most responsible for its beautification. He explained how the *sobhana* qualities of consciousness formed the basis of *bhavana.* He said that generosity was a beautiful quality of consciousness, as were integrity, compassion, love, goodness, truthfulness, composure, and patience.

◆ LIFE IS NEVER ALONE

The elder went on to explain each of the beautiful qualities of consciousness in some depth. But he concluded by saying how *bhavana* was a form of meditation based in life, in world relationships, a concept that made a lasting impression on me. *Bhavana* pointed to an understanding of the dynamics of interpersonal awakening, or what I call finding liberation through living, or, as the South Africans call it, *ubuntu*. He said that the basis of his own Dharma understanding was founded upon the recognition that "life is never alone." We are always in a state of relatedness. In other words, *bhavana* empowers relationships as the most sacred place for awakening.

Cultivating *bhavana* meant extending oneself into the circumstances of any given moment, clearly comprehending those circumstances — *knowing* them — and bringing a liberating intimacy to the space of shared being. "This is how one beautifies consciousness by interrelating with others and the world."

"Life is never alone," he repeated. The more deeply we understand our intrinsic relatedness we see how "liberation is not possible without other people." How could one cultivate generosity without other life to give to? How could one cultivate compassion without opening one's eyes to those who are suffering? How would one ever know the value of integrity unless there was a context to see it and know it when contrasted with deception? Thus, to cultivate *bhavana* one makes each and every encounter with people, with life, with the world, with everything that one does, a moment to beautify being. "This is why the commentaries state, 'make each person you meet your ultimate object of reverence,' " he concluded.

Bhavana is an opening process. It develops in much the same way as a flower opens to the sun. With light, soil, water, and air the flower gradually blossoms and emanates its natural fragrance. It is through *relatedness* that consciousness flowers, not through examining the darkness between the petals. It is not enough to liberate the mind alone. Negative freedom is only one level of the Dharma: freedom from fear, freedom from pride, freedom from this or that tendency. Rather, *bhavana* is an active engagement with the environment of our lives — self with other, self with the world, self with subselves, self with the cosmos. *Bhavana* is an artistry, the ability to expand into the world, to bring color, beauty, and a liberating playfulness to life. *Bhavana* is *ubuntu* and *ubuntu* is *bhavana*. What elevates you elevates me; what denigrates you denigrates me.

World Dharma is guided by wisdom and conscience. Together they serve as an inner compass — an intuitive guide to choose freedom and all things good. As one's Dharma understanding matures, one lives more in alignment with the wisdom of Martin Luther King's words: "All persons are tied in a single garment of destiny. Whatever affects one directly affects all indirectly. . . . I can never be what I ought to be until you are what you ought to be, and you can never be what you ought to be until I am what I ought to be. This is the interrelated structure of reality."

For World Dharma to be real one must see that freedom and caring are intimately interwoven. On the one hand one cares about the quality of one's own being, and on the other, one cares about the quality of life for others. This means that we must enter our inner worlds with our eyes widely focused on the outer world — the interspace of shared being right in front of us, the interrelated present — with people, events, the air, the light.

MUTUAL BEING — US RIGHT NOW!

To me, all ways and means of opening the heart prepare us for the liberating intimacy of mutual being — *us* right now. I call this "interrelated presence," which points to the participatory intelligence that on the one hand honors our uniqueness and on the other respects that we are in relationship to everything all the time.

We don't abandon ourselves to interrelate with others; we awaken to the already present reality of where we meet the world and the world meets us — with the senses, with the mind, with the flesh of our body. Interrelated presence is a basic understanding of ourselves as *being in relationship all the time,* self with subselves, self with others, and self with the world. As a result of this recognition we bring our goodness, intelligence, and creativity to this shared life.

One of my earliest memories of awakening to the wisdom of interrelated presence came many years ago when I lived in Bali. One day my friend Janice invited a friend of hers to visit. When the friend arrived at the house, she brought her brother along. When they walked in I noticed her brother had trouble with his eyes. They looked empty. She explained that her brother, Wayan, was blind and that he'd been unable to see his whole life.

After some tea, Janice and her friend took a walk, leaving me and Wayan on the veranda. After a few minutes of sitting together in silence I noticed that Wayan was smiling. I asked him why.

"Your house is in the country, isn't it?" he asked.

"Yes, it's high up in the country on the side of a steep gorge."

"I can feel it," he said. "I can feel the coolness of the air. I can also hear the sound of the doves in the distance. This is very soothing to me. I live in a one-room apartment in the city. Thank you for having me here."

He paused for a long few moments, and with his smile growing deeper and more reflective, he asked, "May I ask you a question?"

"Sure," I said.

"Would you take me around your home and describe to me what you see? I'd like to enjoy your home the way you see it and enjoy it. In Bali we say that we get to know a person by how they see the world."

I was really touched by his invitation. It was so intimate and real. "Sure," I said. "I'd be honored." I took him by the hand and we stood up and began to slowly walk around the house. I took him to a Buddha statue that had been sitting on an altar over the table for years. As I tried to explain it to him, I realized he didn't ask me to give him a visual tour of things alone but what I enjoyed about these things, how I felt about them, what my relationship was with them. I was sure my silence startled him and so I found myself sharing half-truths, fragmented stories without their complete meaning. He was not asking me to feel sorry for him or to say something that might entertain him. He was inviting me to reveal my heart, to be honest and sensitive to the truth of my experience. It was the oddest thing to realize how inward I had been and how much of my day-to-day environment I had never really noticed, nor really understood or enjoyed. My relatedness to life was selective and narrow and somewhat perfunctory.

When I took him to the upstairs living room, I caught a glimpse of myself in the large mirror against one wall. I wasn't sure where to begin. He picked up on my hesitation and said, "If I am disturbing you I can sit alone until my sister returns." I assured him I was deciding on what to tell him next. He then said in an inviting tone, "May I ask . . . what do you look like?"

I almost started crying on the spot. There was something so utterly naked about this man. While he sat in a chair I looked in the mirror and described myself to him. Although he was blind, he was skilled in bringing vision to light. His profound awareness allowed him, in spite of his injured eyes, to grasp the sensual details of the material world. Instead of continuing to take my own sight for granted, he reminded me and showed me what *my own* eyes see and do. He brought me into our "interrelated presence."

On another occasion, during my first year as a monk in Burma, I learned another precious lesson about tenderness and the wisdom of mutual being — again from someone who didn't take the world for granted. A dear friend, a Burmese monk by the name of U Kundala, had invited me to come out of retreat for a few hours to accompany him on a visit to his aged parents, both of whom lived in an old-age home on the outskirts of Rangoon. This was a few months before the onset of my illnesses.

"I know just where my mother will be," he said in a tone of reverence as we walked into the compound. U Kundala smiled as he pointed to three old women seated on a bench beneath a large orange bougainvillea tree. He grabbed my hand as we walked hurriedly over to the women, introducing me first to his mother, Daw Khin Gyi.

After he and his mother spoke rapidly in Burmese for a minute or so, U Kundala invited me to join in. In halting Burmese I asked the three women their ages.

They laughed. "Young men shouldn't ask old women their age," Daw Khin Gyi said humorously. The fluency of her English startled me as much as her answer.

"I'm sorry," I said, "it's one of the only questions I know in Burmese."

"Well, I'm eighty-two, and my two friends are eighty and eighty-one. And you?" she asked curiously.

"Thirty, my birthday was just a few days ago," I said.

"You're such a young man," she exclaimed. "What are you doing in Burma? Shouldn't you be married, enjoying yourself with your wife?"

Slightly taken aback, I looked toward U Kundala for reassurance, but he had walked off.

"I'm a *pongyi,*" I said, meaning that I was a monk. "I've been living at the Mahasi meditation center with your son. I'm in your country to practice meditation and learn the Dharma."

I concluded somewhat indignantly, "I'm not interested in marriage!"

After a brief moment of silence Daw Khin Gyi asked in a curious voice, "Tell me, since you've become a monk, are you happy?"

"Yeah, sure," I replied without hesitation. "I'm happy. Well, you know... almost. You know how we Buddhists are, never really happy, but always just about there."

The women loved my comment and laughed uproariously. But instead of relaxing, I tensed. Her question made me think. Was I happy? What does that even mean?

I looked down at U Kundala's mother, who was staring at me intently and asked, "And you, are you happy?" No sooner had I finished the question than my heart dropped. I hadn't noticed that she was blind — her eyes were glazed, unblinking, a mass of solid gray. Why hadn't U Kundala told me? No wonder she didn't notice I was a monk.

As I was rebuking myself for asking such an insensitive question, and just about to apologize, she answered with a soft smile,

"Yes, I am happy. Very happy. I have everything I need. Life is good."

It was hard to accept her contentment. Happiness in the best of circumstances seemed so elusive to me. And happiness and blindness, in particular, seemed antithetical. All kinds of thoughts went through my head. Who would I be without sight? My entire existence was conditioned by my ability to see: my hopes, dreams, ambitions, every identity I had about myself and life was tied into my ability to make contact with my eyes. I don't think I had ever considered how conditioned and interrelated my sense of being was until that moment — how utterly dependent I was. I took sight completely for granted, as well as the other senses, and mobility too.

"My friends tell me it's very beautiful here," she continued. "They describe the sunsets — the shades of color, even the stars and the moon, or sometimes a rainbow, or the flight of a bird. My friends are my eyes. But since I've nothing to compare it to it's more like listening to poetry than trying to visualize the scene. But for me beauty comes in other ways."

Her words themselves drifted in the air and seemed illuminated in the late morning sun. A space of being had opened in me beyond my normal awareness of just me. It was as if her words were compelling me to enter a shared space, such as the one she shared with her friends. She broke my reflection with a kind smile and said, "I live simply. What do I need? I take my time when I walk. Where do I need to go? I have my walking stick. I have plenty of food. What more could I ask for? I have a bed in the shelter behind us. I sleep well at night. My clothes are few and comfortable. I stay clean, even though I'm very slow at bathing at the well. If I'm ill, we have herbal medicines." She paused and turned toward me with a sincerity that melted the separation between us. "See, I have all I need," she said, "food, shelter, clothing, and medicines. In Burma we say, these are the four requisites for basic human happiness."

I hadn't noticed that U Kundala had walked up. Next to him was an elderly man bent over, standing with the aid of a cane. Daw Khin Gyi, sensing who it was, said something I didn't understand in Burmese. The elder sat next to her and they held each other's hands. She then looked up at me and said, "But the best thing for happiness is love."

What does it mean to evoke the courage to care about things larger than oneself? How do we recognize that we are in relationship all of the time, that we are a part of something so large and compelling that it inspires us to participate with everything we've got? I think it's worth remembering again the meaning of the word *ubuntu:* "A person becomes a person through other persons." Such a person knows that their humanity, their very existence, is inextricably bound up in others.

◆ THE FUTURE OF FREEDOM

In late 1997, a year after I was blacklisted from reentering Burma, the momentum gathered for me to further understand World Dharma, to try to reconcile it with the darkness around us. I was in Boston toward the end of a three-month-long cross-country speaking tour to raise awareness of the escalating crisis in Burma. Walking back to the hotel that night after my presentation, I followed Boston's Freedom Trail — the historic landmark revealing America's revolutionary roots. Midway along I noticed something up ahead. There were six large luminous glass towers jutting high into the night sky, glowing like tall spectral candles. I crossed the street to investigate. At the base of the first tower there was an inscription carved into the black granite panel: "The New England Holocaust Memorial." Looking skyward I saw swirling strands of smoke coming out of the top of the towers. But these were not towers, they were chimneys — the chimneys of the death camp crematoria.

I turned and walked down the stone pathway passing under the base of the chimneys. As I entered the first one, I heard a calm, clear voice begin to speak over the PA system. It was a taped narration about the memorial, explaining how each of the six-story-high towers was etched — top to bottom — with one million numbers, representing the six million Jews murdered from the time the Nazis came to power in 1933 to their defeat in 1945.

I stopped walking and looked closely at one of the glass towers. Every inch of glass had etched in it a ten-digit number — numbers I assumed the Nazis had branded on the arms of every Jew. I rubbed my finger along a line of numbers — ten symbols, one human. I wondered whom I had touched. Was it a man? A woman? A child? How had they died? Gassed? Worked to death? This number was a human. This number once had a heartbeat. This number had a mother and a father. This number once loved and gave love. This number must have lived a normal life before hell descended. How many times did this person cry? I wondered if he or she ever stopped hoping. When do you stop caring and just give up?

I lowered my hand and walked. After a few steps I stopped again, to look down. At the base of each tower was a large steel grate covering a deep chamber. At the bottom were smoldering coals. Was this room symbolic of the gas chambers where they exterminated people or were they crematoria where their bodies were burned? The coals at the bottom of the pit illuminated the inscriptions on the wall — the names of the six main Nazi death camps: Majdanek, Chelmno, Sobibor, Treblinka, Belzec, and Auschwitz-Birkenau. Six million numbers, six million murdered, and six chimneys coming out of six concentration camps.

I walked on and as I did the narration continued, saying, "Look at these towers, passerby, and try to imagine what they really mean — what they symbolize — what they evoke. They evoke an era of incommensurate darkness, an era in history when civilization lost its humanity and humanity lost its soul."

I kept walking along the pathway under each of the chimneys and stopped under the last one. Standing motionless I became aware of my breathing, and the beating of my heart. Although it was cold out I began to perspire. I then became aware of my flesh, the organs, the blood flowing through the arteries throughout my body — how fragile life is, how each breath makes a tenuous dance with the next. Would this be the last one? Or the next...?

I dropped into the fires below me in an attempt to fathom the ungraspable reality of the Holocaust — inexplicable dimensions of dimensions of darkness. There on the wall beside me I saw the word "REMEMBER" inscribed on black stone. I stood there, struggling to understand. Remember what? What aspect of this great evil shall I remember? How deeply should I take it into my heart? How intimate with reality should I be, I asked myself.

The towers reminded me that human horror originates in the human mind. A mind without conscience is consciousness capable of anything. Should I remember how most people aided the Nazis or simply turned and looked the other way? Should I remember the Nazis murdered one and a half million children? How they castrated homosexuals or used them in macabre medical experiments before they were murdered? How far shall I take this, I asked myself. Are these chimneys here to remind us of the demons in our own mind, and our own potential for aggression? Or was this memorial a reminder of the urgent need for greater self-responsibility? It made me think of Gandhi and how he envisioned the survival of life with his words: "human ... greatness lies not ... in being able to remake the world ... [but] in being able to remake ourselves."

But where would we be today without the weapon? What language exists between the pacifist — nonviolent activists such as Gandhi, King, the Dalai Lama, and Aung San Suu Kyi — and these six million victims, now etched in glass? After my time in Burma, Croatia, and Bosnia, I had become convinced of the legitimate power of a strong military force.

As a means of bringing freedom to his people, Nelson

Mandela substantiated his turn away from nonviolence to violence by citing an old African expression: "the attacks of the wild beast cannot be averted only with bare hands." Nevertheless, some within his political party argued that nonviolence was an inviolate principle, not a tactic that should be abandoned when it no longer worked. To this Mr. Mandela countered, "[I] believed exactly the opposite... [that] it was wrong and immoral to subject our people to armed attacks by the state without offering them some kind of alternative." I couldn't agree more.

America's freedom and my own freedom, too, were achieved only by courage, revolution, and the gun. Perhaps I should be honoring my ancestors who sacrificed their lives for the freedom to stand in this memorial and reflect on the value of that freedom that I love so much.

I was proud to be in America, and a large part of that beauty was the freedom it afforded me to pursue my dreams and to exercise my freedom of speech, thought, and conscience. Equally, I felt saddened at America's numerous shortcomings — the hypocrisies and lies that have created a global scourge through our carnivorous capitalistic corporate culture.

If I am to remember the Holocaust, I had also to remember the hell we created in Vietnam, Nicaragua, and of course, the millions of Native Americans our ancestors destroyed as they stole and settled our motherland. As George Washington so proudly hailed, "freedom is never free."

Is it possible to break the cycle of violence?

I looked down again at the smoldering coals. Questions kept coming to me: Is it possible, or more important, acceptable to allow yourself to frolic in joy while you know the world is ablaze with hatred and war? Is it possible to let in the suffering, and at the same time relax enough to enjoy ordinary human happiness? Can you embrace an awareness of this world — the harsh truth of its horror — without any spin at all? Can you allow for the fact that it is a harsh, brutal landscape where the majority of people are hurting, starving, and anguished — struggling to survive in the most incomprehensibly dark circumstances? Can you live a normal life knowing that these people are your relatives and you are here to help?

It's no wonder people seek nirvana — a place of perfection beyond name, time, and horror. It's no wonder guru worship, projection, and other forms of pseudospiritual escape are so popular. To feel so much is overwhelming. Did the path of compassion, therefore, need to be tempered with escape, whether in the form of faith, myth, or pharmaceuticals? Not very spiritually correct thinking, but neither was the God behind the Holocaust.

The truth is simple — we are in a circumstance where anything can happen, and does. Every second is a mysterious twist of infinite cosmic fate, and our individual lives refract a microscopic unit of the immensity. And if I'm not hiding in delusion, then I am forcing myself to stand in the naked nirvana of reverential uncertainty, occupying as many dimensions of being as my heart can bear and has the wisdom to inhabit. If I can stand here, I'm standing in pure awareness of life, without the distorting filters that distance me from that which I am: an open space, large and small, fragile and strong, deep and shallow, vulnerable and powerful, unprotected, naked, mortal, and completely mysterious. No one knows who they are, really. We may be anything. We may be everything. The point is, not to fix on one thing or the other.

Within this understanding I needed nothing. No faith apart from a trust in my deepest experience of being — in love, right now. It then dawned on me that I was standing in my own truth, freely — my flawed, wonderful self. Although the coals were still flaming beneath me, I began to smile. Now what? Listen to the voice within you, came the answer. Listen to your conscience. *Don't be afraid of the universe.*

I walked out from underneath the last chimney. As I did I noticed another granite panel, which read: "This statement, attributed to Pastor Martin Niemoeller, has become a legendary expression of the Holocaust."

They came first for the Communists,
And I didn't speak up because I wasn't a Communist.
Then they came for the Jews,
And I didn't speak up because I wasn't a Jew.
Then they came for the trade unionists,
And I didn't speak up because I wasn't a trade unionist.
Then they came for the Catholics,
And I didn't speak up because I was a Protestant.
Then they came for me,
And by that time no one was left to speak up.

Conscience — the courage to feel our innate interrelatedness — is so precious. My heart tells me that the true Dharma life is to care about things larger than oneself. I faced the towers and lowered my head in gratitude. I then walked back to the hotel with the word "remember" flowing through my heart. Yes, remember that we're in this thing together, that we can't do it alone.

Listening to conscience is to discern what is real, true, and good from what is unreal, unbeneficial, and untrue. This process continually nourishes our dignity. Responding to conscience is one fundamental way of finding liberation through living. Conscience, choice, and freedom grow from one another, and in doing so they perpetuate a cycle of freedom.

The more freedom one has, the greater the perspective on life. The more space, the more responsibility we feel to take part in the lives of others. From here the stakes get higher and the decisions more complex. Our responsibility increases. Conscience asks that we care about life, and wisdom tells us to act. The future of freedom is in our hands, each and every day of our lives.

THE REAWAKENING OF BEAUTY

"Beauty will save the world," Dostoevsky once wrote. The idea is, in itself, beautiful, but *how* will it save the world? Is there an understanding of beauty that can assuage the heart of fear and end oppression? Is there a form of beauty that exceeds all others — a universal beauty that is the essence of life?

Beauty is so many things. It's a feeling. To be stirred in one's heart is beautiful. It is beautiful to see courage triumph over adversity. To feel solidarity with someone else's struggle is beautiful. Kindness and loyalty are beautiful. Certain states of consciousness are beautiful, too. Struggling for what one believes in is beautiful. Standing up for the greater good is beautiful. Reconciliation and anything that interrupts a self-denigrating habit are beautiful. Overcoming complacency is beautiful. People, art, a poem, a smile, a photograph — anything that provokes or stimulates us to inhabit a new aspect of reality is beautiful. And peace might be the greatest beauty of all.

Francis, my homeless friend from Montreal, who's been living nearby for the past few years, is a beautiful man. I don't know what array of unfortunate circumstances landed him on the street, but he lives out there with remarkable composure. He occasionally gives me flowers and nice little rocks and small things he makes and carves. And he never complains at all. Not even when it has rained for five days straight in the near-freezing winter and he's shivering and sopping wet. Not Francis. I asked him the secret to his freedom the other day. He smiled and said, "You meditate... I'm just me." We had a good laugh over that one. That's our local Saint Francis, our local beautiful mind. I admire his natural way of being in the world.

Is the kind of beauty that Francis shows me the sort that can save the terrible mess our world is in? I think it's a start. But how does street beauty speak to the big picture? And, furthermore, how does the big picture speak to street beauty? Although I can appreciate that the biological intelligence orchestrating the hundred billion neurons in our brains right now is inseparable from the quantum intelligence that unifies every wave and particle of existence in the cosmos, it's difficult for me to embrace that reality as truly beautiful. It is as it is — phenomenal existence. We are all finite organic systems, unique and conscious of ourselves, while configured within this infinitely mysterious coherence. This majesty is interesting but also terrifying. From this perspective beauty is no longer continuous with a sense of enchantment. The big picture does not guarantee wonder. This is because this quantum intelligence — this universal interplay of principles — has also to account for the devastating ugliness of genocide, famine, and human stupidity.

Perhaps we can think of beauty in terms of basic human intelligence, a way of being that is respectful toward all of life while also vigilant in maintaining human freedom. When this liberating way of being is repeated often enough, by more and more people, it is the beauty that can save the world. It is a beauty that transcends religion, nationality, and doctrine.

Could there be anything more sacred, more immediate, more beautiful than freedom? Take away someone's basic human rights, one's freedom, and generally speaking, they suffer the greatest loss. For me it is nearly unimaginable what it would mean not to be able to move about freely, or to speak openly, or to practice my form of spirituality, for fear of imprisonment or harm. Even for a day, it's hard to imagine.

Nelson Mandela — the great pillar of strength and wisdom that he is — said that during the twenty-six years he spent in a South African prison that "I thought continually of the day when I would walk free." He proclaims freedom as the highest good — a quality so beautiful that no fear is too large to confront in the struggle. No fear — not the fear of being maimed, of imprisonment, of torture, or even of death — would stand in the way of his commitment to freedom. "Our message," he declared, "was that no sacrifice was too great in the struggle for freedom."

FREEDOM IS ITS OWN REWARD

When I was last in Burma in 1996 I got a deep look at unmediated freedom — a courageous freedom expressed in the immediacy of the moment. I had been invited by Aung San Suu Kyi to her home in Rangoon to celebrate her country's Independence Day. The event had special significance. Although Burma had gained its freedom from Britain in 1947, in a strange and tragic twist of fate, for the previous four decades the population has been brutally oppressed by Burma's own army.

So, in an act of defiance to the military dictators ruling the country, Aung San Suu Kyi and other elected leaders of the democracy movement called for a celebration of their "inherent freedom" at her home. To counter this, the regime's generals threatened long prison terms for anyone attending. But in the spirit of revolution the three hundred or so people who came out that day showed up more emboldened than ever. The more they were threatened, the more their determination grew. As Martin Luther King Jr. said, "Only when it's dark out do you see the stars."

As the festivities were about to begin, several thousand more people gathered on University Avenue — the road just outside Aung San Suu Kyi's compound. Large loudspeakers were hooked up to broadcast the celebration to everyone on the street. Tensions increased as policemen walked among the crowds of activists, filming everyone in attendance. Everyone present faced the harsh reality that when they went home that day they could be arrested and have their homes confiscated.

I stood looking out over the crowd, thinking about what it meant to really stand up for what you believe in. Here I understood more clearly Aung San Suu Kyi's words: "Within a system which denies the existence of basic human rights, fear tends to be the order of the day. Fear of imprisonment, fear of torture, fear of death; fear of losing friends, family, property or means of livelihood; fear of poverty, fear of isolation, fear of failure. The most insidious form of fear is that which masquerades as common sense or even wisdom, condemning as foolish, reckless, insignificant, or futile the small, daily acts of courage which help to preserve a person's self-respect and inherent human dignity."

It's the little moments, the details of life, the immediacy of freedom's function — to be free right now — that excite me the most. *Freedom is its own reward.* By occupying freedom it grows, organically. Every second is a creative choice to exercise freedom — our greatest beauty. What we do with that freedom will change, but the more we release the energy of freedom from the constraint of conditions, the more liberated we become. Imagine being a pianist or a potter and losing our hands? Imagine then getting them back? Imagine the gratitude we would feel for the freedom that our hands provide us? The idea is to have our hands and hearts on life all the time — aware that we can lose that privilege at any time — playing and shaping the rhythms and forms that most touch us.

By midafternoon the Independence Day celebration was in full swing. There were theatrical presentations from each of the different ethnic groups of Burma's fourteen states. The music, dance, and joy of solidarity were all the more poignant taking place in a present moment that had no guarantee of a future.

People celebrated in full knowledge that they may not see each other again after that day. The prisons were already full with activists who had done much less to provoke the authorities. And before long, as expected, hundreds of armed soldiers loyal to the dictatorship surrounded Aung San Suu Kyi's compound. Dozens of paddy wagons moved in and barricaded the street.

As the soldiers surrounded us, waiting ominously, the master of ceremonies announced a special guest. The audience went silent in anticipation. As the curtains on the makeshift stage opened the audience roared, recognizing Burma's most famous stand-up comedian, U Par Lay, and his partner, U Lu Zaw. Together they formed a theater troupe called Myo Win Mar, or "Our Own Way." Comics in Burma are spoken-word artists in the fullest sense. They combine storytelling, dance, acting, impersonation, humor, philosophy, drama, Dharma, wit, and political satire that express the conscience of the nation. It becomes a form of radical activism. In Burma, a country where speaking freely is a crime against the state, the spoken-word performer faces something like what Lenny Bruce faced in the late 1950s and early 1960s in America but immeasurably worse.

The last time U Par Lay and U Lu Zaw had performed, in 1989, they were imprisoned for six years. They were shackled in leg irons, forced to pound rocks every day, deprived of medicine and visits by family members, and kept on a near-starvation diet. Their crime: mildly satirizing the Big Brother behavior of Burma's totalitarian regime.

When the audience saw their favorite performers on stage — who they did not know had just been released from prison — they responded with electrified, deafening applause. U Par Lay took the microphone and explained that he had been waiting for this day for six years — the day when he would be free again to stand up, perform, and speak his conscience.

He said he knew that what he was about to perform would land him back in prison. After another huge round of applause, with a defiant smile U Par Lay said, "So be it! It's about our freedom!"

I tried to imagine the implications of his actions. I visualized him in prison chained in leg irons, along with the hundreds of other political prisoners, standing under a sweltering sun, hungry and emaciated, swinging a heavy sledge hammer over his head and then down against rock. And to think that he's smiling inside? He so evidently sustained himself through his love of freedom — his commitment to human rights, his dedication to liberation through living. He must have, somehow, always remembered that his freedom is inseparable from everyone else's.

As I listened and watched U Par Lay, I felt the courage of the crowd around me. They too were risking it all for freedom. I began to breathe more deeply. I began to laugh more fully. I occupied my body and my muscles and my skin in a more natural, liberated way. I was no longer an outsider looking in. I wasn't a practitioner of any religion or meditation seeking freedom. I was a human being. I was in the flow of a timeless freedom, unbound by fear, unbound by location, unbound by nationality, creed, and religion. As U Par Lay declared his freedom by being true to himself, I too became free in my own unique form of activism. My interrelated presence was all that I ever had. A love of mutual being was my only message.

As I occupied more of my own heart and less of my fear, I automatically felt greater care for others. People got up and started to dance. They had no rhythm to follow other than their own love of freedom. U Par Lay was telling us through his example, "Don't wait to be." He was saying, "Open the window and look at the stars. Don't let dictators tell you what liberation looks like, or what the sacred should feel like." U Par Lay was being himself, and at the same time inextricably connected to the larger picture — his country's struggle for freedom, his country's uprising for human rights, the freedom to say and be who you want to be, right now.

It is frighteningly easy to empower compromise. It is so easy to postpone freedom until circumstances improve. It is so easy to seek the idea rather than empower the little, daily acts of manifesting dreams. In the bigger picture it would be easy to dismiss U Par Lay's actions as having no real value. It would be easy to forget the millions of other people around the world who risk so much every day of their lives for the right to a dignified existence. How many U Par Lays are there out there in the making? How many Francises?

Vaclav Havel, who spent years in prison for his activism in helping to bring freedom to his country, once said, "Hope, in the deep and meaningful sense, is not the same as joy that things are going well, or willingness to invest in enterprises that are obviously headed for early success, but, rather, an ability to work for something because it is good, not just because it stands a chance to succeed." Freedom is about the elevation of this human goodness. This beauty will save the world, if we are patient and persevering. "People who are used to seeing society only from above tend to be impatient," Havel went on to say. "They want to see immediate results. Anything that does not produce immediate results seems foolish. They don't have a lot of sympathy for acts which can only be evaluated years after they take place, which are motivated by moral factors, and therefore run the risk of never accomplishing anything."

Mother Teresa spoke to the heart of World Dharma when she said, "We cannot do great things in life; we can only do small things with great love." Saving the world will come from hundreds of millions of people performing the tiniest acts throughout the day with the "great love" Mother Teresa speaks of. That great love is born from a love of freedom, our own and others. As Nelson Mandela states, "For to be free is not merely to cast off one's chains, but to live in a way that respects and enhances the freedom of others."

Once we embrace the reality that our freedom cannot be separated, our devotion to it begins. So U Par Lay and U Lu Zaw demonstrated back on January 4, 1996. They performed beautifully. It was a very mild satirical commentary, highlighting a few of the fatal flaws of an unjust, misguided system that out of greed and fear oppresses all of human life. The audience within Aung San Suu Kyi's compound cried and laughed. And sure enough, a few days later U Par Lay and U Lu Zaw were rearrested, sentenced without a trial, once again, to six years of rock pounding. A two-hour gig to celebrate unbound freedom cost them six years.

The regime in Burma is profoundly ugly, corrupt at every level, but the effort to speak to that ugliness, to declare it wrong, is a beautiful act of conscience. That's *ubuntu*. That's *bhavana*. That's World Dharma. That's liberation through living.

Sometimes when I watch children playing I imagine hearing them say in their innocence, "Please make the world a beautiful place. We want to grow up safe and free." The challenge is before us, always present — a living universe — waiting for us each to creatively occupy it — wisely, openly, curiously, free. This is the Dharma: a daring declaration of our devotion to liberation by exploring consciousness and the relationship of the human to both world and cosmos.

Am I optimistic? Let Nelson Mandela answer that question. "I am fundamentally an optimist. Whether that comes from nature or nurture, I cannot say. Part of being optimistic is keeping one's head pointed toward the sun, one's feet moving forward. There were many dark moments when my faith in humanity was sorely tested, but I would not and could not give myself up to despair. That way lay defeat and death."

LOVE SETS US FREE

"Security is mostly a superstition, it does not exist in nature, nor do the children... as a whole experience it. Avoiding danger is no safer in the long run than outright exposure. Life is either a daring adventure or nothing at all." This quote by Helen Keller offers us a powerful reminder of the importance of seizing our life right now, and challenging the forces of limitation.

We exist on earth for a brief time. Life is an experience that is always interrupted. What would it feel like to be in the final days of our life? It's certainly happening, whether we think it is or not. How empty and precious everything would seem — as it actually is — if we knew that today was all we had.

I think of my friend Liliane in Sydney, Australia, who at thirty was diagnosed with an inoperable cancer. Her response was a stunning and courageous example of *ubuntu* and *bhavana*. After her diagnosis, her doctor compassionately discouraged her from chemotherapy, giving her three to four weeks to live. But Liliane refused to die without a fight. Every weekend she would go to the hospital for treatment and from Monday through Wednesday she would vomit and be so sick and weak she couldn't get out of bed. Never once did she complain or lose hope. Thursdays were the only day of the week she was strong enough to walk, before going back into the hospital on Friday for forty-eight more hours of chemotherapy.

I remember every Thursday walking with her slowly along the beach in the windy chill of winter. Every Thursday Liliane would undress on the spot and jump into the frigid ocean. I remember telling myself that I wouldn't do that even if I were the one dying. Her spontaneity and fearlessness were in themselves a magnificent teaching. Liliane turned her illness into a gift for herself and those of us who were blessed to be near her. She smiled at strangers, and even asked sometimes if they cared to stop and talk for a few minutes. It was her one free day a week and she used it completely. She would dance on the beach, and sometimes fall over because she was so weak. She would sing children's songs to the sea gulls as we walked. She would hang out with the homeless and ask them questions about their lives. She cared more about life each week, despite her doctor's insistence that she stop hoping because there was no hope. She didn't stop. Eventually we did stop going to the beach on Thursdays. Instead, she went back to the hospital and comforted the women in her cancer ward who were also terminal. Liliane lives today. She thinks it was her love of relationship that saved her life, the healing power of *ubuntu* and *bhavana,* that of liberating intimacy.

World Dharma points to the power of engaging our human interrelatedness with wisdom, compassion, and creative integrity as the basis of developing freedom and dignity. The wisdom of World Dharma is carried in this comment by Nelson Mandela: "It was during those long and lonely years [in prison] that my hunger for the freedom of my own people became a hunger for the freedom of all people, white and black. I knew as well as I knew anything that the oppressor must be liberated just as surely as the oppressed. A man who takes away another man's freedom is a prisoner of hatred, he is locked behind the bars of prejudice and narrow-mindedness. I am not truly free if I am taking away someone else's freedom, just as surely as I am not free when my freedom is taken from me. The oppressed and the oppressor alike are robbed of their humanity. When I walked out of prison, that was my mission, to liberate the oppressed and the oppressor both."

Liberation through living comes alive to the extent that we feel ourselves as contextual beings. Our every second of life depends on forces both internal and external. We are simultaneously unique and indistinguishable from the whole. We are everywhere at once and at the same time challenged to come to terms with our apparent separateness and mortality.

The awakening of liberation through living accelerates from a deep recognition of relatedness. There is a shift from my separateness, my circle of friends, my *sangha,* my family, my community, my nation — into the beauty of being related wherever you are, even when alone.

A few days before I was forced to leave Burma in March 1996, I met with my dear friend U Tin Oo. We had been monks together in the early 1980s. He was now the chairman of the National League for Democracy, the political party of which Aung San Suu Kyi serves as general secretary. He is yet another wise and courageous statesman who was imprisoned under unimaginable conditions. I asked him what it took to emotionally and psychologically survive the severity of eleven years of prison and solitary confinement. His answer lives with me today as essential to World Dharma.

"Oh, I had ways to keep my spirit alive," he said with a beautiful boyish smile lifting his radiant seventy-six-year-old face. "My hut within the prison was detached from the main cells and was encircled with barbed wire. I was indoors all the time, and the wire was a constant reminder of how precious freedom was. Like in the Buddha's Dharma teachings, obstacles can be seen as advantages; the loss of one's freedom can inspire the reflection on the preciousness of freedom. This filled me with joy.

"Also, I knew from my years as a practicing monk the benefits of *sati* — mindfulness meditation. Just do everything you do with awareness and there is no room in one's mind for negative thoughts. I approached every day in prison as I did as a monk in the monastery, mindfully. I tried to notice everything that occurred in my mind and body: everything you see, hear, taste, think, and smell becomes simply an experience, without anything extra placed upon it. Just phenomena. So in that way, too, the thought of imprisonment is seen as just a thought. It comes and goes. And without attachment to it there's no problem. It's just a thought. In this way I could keep my mind free of afflictive emotions.

"I would also regularly recite the Buddha's discourses in Pali as well as study them, which inspired me greatly. In addition, a small book containing quotations of Jesus was smuggled through to me. I very much liked his attitude of forgiveness and sincerity.

"Also, I made it a habit to give *dana* — the offering of a gift — to my jailers. I wanted to overcome any feelings of seeing them as the enemy so I tried to make it a practice of sharing a little of my food with them. They, too, had a hard life in prison. This eased my emotional and psychological pain to some extent.

"I abstained from taking food after midday. There are many people in my country who are hungry due to the policies of this dictatorship. By not eating after noon I remained in solidarity with them."

He paused and closed his eyes for a moment. Then he opened them, saying, "But most importantly I would reflect on the preciousness of my friendships. So in moments of difficulty I would envision their faces one by one and talk to them a bit. I would recall our moments of laughter and the joys we shared."

He then turned to me and held both my hands with his own, and with a warm tender smile said, "It's the love that you feel that keeps your sanity. It's the love that sets you free."

This story reminds me of the importance of our shared presence, the importance of bringing the very best qualities of my being to the moments of my life — alone and in the company of others.

I ask myself as often as I need to: Can I renew my courage to love? Can I be in direct communion with myself, others, and the world, simultaneously? We are in this together. We need each other to actualize our full potential to love, our full potential to liberate ourselves and each other, together, as we evolve life into the future.

To embrace the Dharma requires that we envelop life in this very moment as all we have. From such an awakened state of presence we are free to live and die, ready to touch and be touched.

◆ TO BE TOUCHED

Whether someone admits it or not doesn't matter, I think everyone wants to be touched — physically, emotionally, and spiritually. Everyone wants to be loved. To be heard. To feel special. People want to be swept off their feet — erotically vibrant with all circuits go. How beautiful it is to be with someone who genuinely adores you, who wants to know everything you think and feel. They delight in you. They celebrate you, draw you out, contact the most sexy, gorgeous, and evocative places in your heart and mind. Imagine becoming someone who is radically willing to be the love they seek, to be the chemistry they long for, to be alive — right now — rather than walking around hungry for what they see as missing from their lives.

To be touched by one's own life may well be one of the greatest miracles of all. Can we ignite the miracle of love in us, so much so that we kindle an awe of being alive — as tender and fragile as we are? Is it possible, at this time, with all we know, to be that bowled over? Where exactly is the wisdom that compels us to rethink our priorities, our attitudes — the entire way we hold the world, ourselves, and our relationships? How do we learn to feel something with every ounce of our being? Is it something we can learn?

My poetic entry into an intimate relationship with Jeannine, in 1998, revealed to me the beauty of a very special love. We had met in Vancouver during the last leg of my book tour for *The Voice of Hope*. What impressed me about Jeannine was her range of deep interests and her love of learning. We were pulled together, in part, because of our mutual passion for Dharma and freedom, and yet, even still, none of it was what I could have expected. In a way, it is exactly this kind of chemistry that is required to feel the innocence at the core of who we are. Two months into our relationship we were living in Hawaii, on the island of Kauai. At first, it felt indulgent, indeed almost unthinkable, to be frolicking in tropical paradise. It was such a dramatic departure from my previous years of war zones and activism. But Jeannine's intuition was that it was exactly what I needed to release me from the emotional hardening I had experienced.

It was a spectacular time. We laughed and played and made love. But I didn't know I would come undone. Through a combination of Jeannine's depth and the healing power of nature, I experienced a reawakening — the release of a vulnerability and a sense of goodness in myself that had been suppressed by deep inner pain. I had responded to the world — the trauma of injustice, war, and the death of friends — with antidepressants, nicotine, and numbness. I didn't see those techniques as inherently wrong. They simply seemed like a means of survival. I used them to assuage the ravaged areas of my heart scarred by trauma and grief.

I always knew in my soul I would let go of these coping devices at the right time. Well, Jeannine helped bring me into that time. Though it's difficult to isolate the exact moment your heart moves, there is no doubt that these transitions occur and as a result we are changed. Generally, moments of great psychological and spiritual transition are marked by mystery, intimacy, and a kind of mystical grace.

One evening under the full moon, with the ocean so still, we decided to paddle out in a kayak. About a half mile offshore we stopped, surprised to see that we were surrounded by a gentle rippling movement on the surface of the ocean. It was a magnificent pod of whales, their shiny ebony backs moving in and out of the water's dark surface in unbroken harmony. And in that moment, under the moonlight, and with the sweet joy that comes from being in the presence of someone you love, I felt something deep in myself relax. Unknowingly, I had been braced — held in by a tension, a sadness, a hurt. I leaned my head back and looked up at the stars — a galaxy of shimmering lights against a backdrop of infinity. I saw the years that had held the pain and suffering of people I loved, the sadness of a world in so much chaos, the ways my own needs and fears had created a numbness that had kept me from a more intimate freedom. The stories of my life paraded by — a stream of struggles and sadnesses, across the immeasurable universe. Just then Jeannine turned around and smiled so gently, as if to indicate that she knew and understood. There was nowhere to go but to let go. I just dropped the stories I had been painfully holding onto. Despite the horrors of the world, I said to myself, let this love set you free. I wanted to live, not die. Under the moon, as we climbed out of time, I cried. From that moment on, I reentered a deeper me, a more available me — a new, more beautiful sense of natural freedom.

By the end of our time in Hawaii I decided that I wanted to return to my greatest love — sharing the Dharma, lecturing and leading meditation retreats. It had been nearly seven years since I had begun my sabbatical from teaching. I attribute this unexpected opening to the power of love, the love I felt for Jeannine, and the love I felt for being true to my instinct for freedom.

One quality I adore more than any other is bringing one's most open, vital self to the moment and interrelating with those who are present with all of one's heart and soul. If the liberating wisdom of shared presence is to be real and made manifest, it needs to be realized, enacted, and explored through the pores of our being. We need to enter simultaneous space without any desire to escape.

What entering shared space means in actuality is for each of us to discover. What I have noticed is when separation dissolves, "my presence" and "their presence" converges. The Dharma becomes a liberating dance of honor, kindness, and goodness rather than a solo act of "me being aware of me alone." I let go into life, feeling my way in, rather than "observing, witnessing, or mirroring phenomena" alone. Occupying ordinary mutuality removes the need for a transcendent agenda. It brings us into the moment for no other purpose than to be together. And that togetherness doesn't even have to be particularly spiritual. Naturalness is enough.

It has been my experience that the less contrived I am, the less beholden to an image of being, the more caring and ethical I become. Why? Naturalness brings out the best in us. At the center of naturalness is love, for self and others.

◆ THE NATURAL LIFE

Natural freedom is not a separate, exclusive condition. It is an all-encompassing vision of the world as a whole, the human as a whole, the cosmos as a whole, the holy whole. One doesn't discover freedom, one presumes it, breathes it, lives it, *is* it. Natural freedom is instinctual. It is beyond qualifications, outcomes, and strategies. It is expressed exactly in the same way you kiss. Can you engage life as naturally as you kiss? When we kiss, or when we smile, we are free, for a moment, from conflict. Our awareness and presence are dedicated to a creative expression of intimacy. The dilemma of looking into the past or the future for some idea of a resolution to the present is gone, not by some strategy, but through the sensuous particularity offered by the kiss itself. Can you abandon yourself to life that fully, and really *know* that freedom is identical to living the Dharma?

The wisdom of the natural life sees that there is no indestructible realization to seek, no final solution to existence, no goal of life, and no required insight apart from the wisdom to be true to yourself and respectful of others. When you relax supernatural fantasies of escaping existence or attaining some perfect truth, you gradually make peace with being in your body, in life, now. Natural freedom makes no more excuses; one is free to fall in love with life again. From this revitalizing innocence one is tender and gentle as well as raw and immediate.

There is no spirituality to seek; it is the very nature of life. It is as innate to existence as the breath. One doesn't need to learn to breathe. One doesn't need to become more spiritual or less material. We only need to be inspired to do something remarkable with the vitality that a full breath provides us. Once we start embodying the magnificent, weird beauty of being hyperconscious, biologically encased creatures, we begin to live more creative, engaged lives. We look at things differently. We hold ourselves with more dignity. We listen to the voices of instinct and intuition more carefully. We use our imagination more. We dream more freely. We take greater risks. Simply, we are more dynamic because we are no longer afraid that we are somehow in the wrong place, or that there is some better place to manifest the Dharma.

For me, natural freedom most spontaneously arises when I cease seeing myself as a separate entity looking out at an external world. This is like a timeless conversation, or like making love. At some point when we make love we cease worrying about how close or far apart we are with our partner. When we cease occupying centrality and abide in mutuality we go from being two individuals to a flow or a dance of energy. Boundaries cease to have the fixed meaning we normally assign them. If there is deep trust, inside and outside, the self and other blend into an intimate unity from human to quantum, from sweat to silence, from eroticism to stillness. It is my sense that when we make love we effect totality. How could we not, when that is who we are?

Transcendent perfection is beyond this world. We reach for this ideal state, cleansing ourselves of human corruptions through the rigor of spiritual discipline, balanced effort, and patient practice. To imagine and aspire and dream perfection is one thing. But there is a catch: we are merely human. It is paradoxical but that humanity is precisely what makes it so worthwhile.

Recognizing our innate mutuality helps to dissolve the given dichotomy between ideal and real, between inside and outside. Why divide the playground between profane and sacred? Why participate in the spiritual apartheid of *my* religion? There is more instinctive music than comparing oneself to a hierarchical gradation of spiritual understanding based on ancient doctrines and modern translators. The Dharma is not a dance contest. No one is measuring the quantity of air we are breathing.

There is no predetermined program that will guarantee your own happiness. It would be like someone telling you what an orgasm should feel like. Should it be transpersonal or personal? Should it be Buddhist or Jewish? Should it be self-involved or should it be absent of self? Should it be in this world or beyond this world? Should I worry about mine, or my lack of one, or should I see myself as natural? Should I be thinking or should a real one take me beyond thought? Am I being spiritual when I have an orgasm or am I avoiding my higher self? The ways in which we discriminate between this or that are endless. Seeking perfection is a full-time job, and a thankless one. You will always be graded by a lie: your own unwillingness to be you — human. Perfect has to be reinvented every moment.

LIVING AS A FREE HUMAN BEING

I remember saying good-bye to my grandmother at her home in Boston in 1979, on my way to Burma to ordain as a monk. I was in my late twenties at the time and she was eighty-four. I loved her as much as any one in the world. Having lived with her off and on during my youth, I was provided with a rare glimpse of true love. Now she was old and I was uncertain when I would return from Asia. Although we didn't say it, we both somehow understood that we were saying good-bye.

Toward the end of the day she brought out an old album of photographs. Sitting on the sofa next to me she opened the album worn with age. On the first page, there was a family photograph. "Who is that?" I asked. She placed her finger on the young woman in the photo and said, "That's your nana when she was seventeen. And that's your grandfather next to me. And in my arms is your first aunt, Olga. Your grandfather and I took a steamer from Europe to New York City. I was still in my wedding dress. This picture is from 1913, one year after we arrived."

As we sat there in silence I could see her probing deep into the image. My grandfather had died some years back, as had five of her seven sisters, as well as two of her seven daughters. As I looked back down at the photo, she reached out and held my hand. Her fingers were gnarled and crooked from arthritis. I reflected on how much I had loved staying with her, the walks through the forest, picking blueberries and grapes from her vines, her teaching me how to cook, telling me stories from her childhood, and always showering me with kindness and respect.

I don't know what had gone through her mind as she traveled over those seventy years of her life, but I could see she had been touched when a tear ran down her cheek. She pursed her lips, shook her head slightly, and said, "It feels like just last week."

As she walked me to the door to say good-bye, she looked at me with the most radiant smile, then gently placed her aged hand over my heart. "It's all right there, in your own heart," she said. We hugged and wept and said good-bye three or four times, in the kind of way that people do when they know they will never see each other again. It was one of the most difficult moments of my life, but farewell it was, and off I went, waving and waving good-bye.

The wisdom of my grandmother's words have, over the years, resonated as deep as any spiritual teaching I've learned since. To be true to oneself must be among the most radical acts possible. Why? Because it subverts the mechanisms of conformity. In Burma, when I asked U Kyi Maung, my friend and mentor who spent eleven years in solitary confinement, what the Dharma meant to him in prison, he simply replied, "As a prisoner of conscience my freedom was not my captors to take." Aung San Suu Kyi said it this way: "The only real prison is fear, and the only real freedom is freedom from fear."

Being true to oneself confronts the status quo of our own fear, and whatever external circumstances onto which we project that fear. Only when I am really myself on the deepest, most dignified level, do I grow and change. I have slowly discovered that I am my own best teacher. My compass is my conscience. My instincts are my best friend. And they are always there. Dharma intelligence is another way of talking about conscience mixed with courage, compassion, and instincts. Dharma intelligence is a natural quality of trusting your deepest experience — a core knowing beneath personas and defenses and stories of loss or fear, beneath every compromising trick of the mind and veil of self-deception. Dharma intelligence is an intuitive flow of liberating presence that keeps freeing us every day, every way. That's being true to oneself. That's attuning to one's instinct for freedom.

Meditation taught me that no two moments of perception are the same. Henry Miller said, "The moment one gives close attention to anything, even a blade of grass, it becomes a mysterious, awesome, indescribably magnificent world in itself." The flowering of the heart, of freedom, is the same.

The essence of freedom is naturalness. That means that no two of us find liberation the same way. No two of us will "be natural" in the same way. Watch yourself dance and you'll see what I mean. Look at the way you write. Or smile. Or walk. Or talk. Uniqueness is the quality that makes freedom so fragrant. That's the challenge for the ten thousand employees working in front of a computer at Microsoft, or the thousands of workers on an assembly line at General Motors, or the millions of faithful Buddhist monks and nuns living around the world. "No work is insignificant," Martin Luther King Jr. said, reminding us of the power of fusing dignity, naturalness, and freedom. "All labor that uplifts humanity has dignity and importance and should be undertaken with painstaking excellence. If a man is called to be a street sweeper, he should sweep the streets even as Michelangelo painted, or Beethoven composed music, or Shakespeare wrote poetry. He should sweep the streets so well that all the hosts of heaven and earth will pause to say: 'Here lived a great street sweeper who did his job well.' "

Freedom begins as an approach that can open us to another way of living altogether. Freedom is willing to take risks. "Forget safety. Live where you fear to live. Destroy your reputation. Be notorious," wrote Rumi. He was a mystical outlaw, who refused to be embedded in the concrete of conformity. In the same way, by being true to her innate dignity and beauty, Rosa Parks snapped a lot of white people out of the conforming trance of their racial prejudice. My teachers in Burma were inner pioneers. The demonstrators in Tiananmen Square were heroes and heroines of freedom. Martin Luther King Jr. gave us all a reason to dream. What will it be?

Living the revolutionary life has its risks. And yes, there are numerous obstacles that keep one from going for it — from embracing one's calling or from compromising the pace of its expression. Some will call going after your dreams fanciful thinking. Others will sneer, and try to dress you up in their own negative self-image, calling you self-indulgent, hinting that you're not talented enough to achieve your aim. Clearly, we do not need to conform to someone else's definition of us, nor hide in the neurotic comfort of another's projection. It is my belief that if we really want something from our lives, we've got to go for it — give it our best and make it happen.

People often tell me that they do not know who they are or what it is that ignites their soul. "How do I know the real me," they ask, "the most authentic, passionate expression of my innermost being?" I believe that each of us has a special talent, a unique gift, a skill, a strength that is our very own, whatever it may be. However deep it may be buried, no matter how unclear it may be in the moment, the fact remains — a treasure is in your chest. The spiritual journey, ongoing spiritual practice, should include this continuing awakening to our passions.

Of course, everything has its own time. There can be urgency, but life can't be rushed. In that sense, life must feed itself. As Gandhi said, "Victory is in the struggle itself." But struggle is not the only thing that life has to offer. Sure, life hurts, but it has been my experience that after we've learned all that we can from the hardship and the pain — after we've hurt and cried and ranted long enough — we get back to the beautiful business of making our dream come true.

The spiritual life should not be mistaken for a totalitarian imagination where one style fits all. There is no look that one should adopt. Humans are divine beings, not entities to program into automatons, or manufacture as mannequins that serve the needs of the elite. Slavery, forced or self-induced, is a crime. The Dharma frees one from that which is folded, for the same reason as the poet Rainer Maria Rilke stated: "for where I am closed I am false."

Finding our liberation through living involves deep personal trust in the inherent rightness of our humanness and our natural intelligence. We are not concerned with angling toward or away from any one state or the other, whether it be silence or sound, movement or stillness, being or doing, freedom or bondage, the personal or the transpersonal. Natural freedom embraces our broken human wholeness, and consciously stops attempting to synchronize with perfection. The most perfect people inevitably have the narrowest outlooks. Self-images are like that. Even the most transparent are suits of armor. Like cellophane, you can see through them, but unless you unwrap from them you can't get out.

The Dharma also allows us to become undone. What would be the point of liberation if it didn't free us — to create, to be ourselves, to be real, to enjoy the divinity of this remarkable world that we are just waking up to? With natural freedom we come to really know that even mistakes, even breakdowns, are preferable to artificial behavior. We know the importance of imagination, of creativity. We know the importance of openness — not settling on conclusions about wholeness, awakening, freedom.

The Dharma requires only a resounding trust in the inherent sanctity of our being. There are so many ways to enhance the dance — ways to stretch, push ourselves, release contraction, relax struggle, engender humor, and interrelate with greater wisdom. The Dharma is a metaphor for freedom, not a doctrine that can be memorized and followed step-by-step. While some forms of dance follow rules, the Dharma plays on the floor of infinite moves.

Live your life and struggle to be who you want to be. This is my best philosophical and spiritual advice about how to find liberation. There is no higher Dharma outside of this. It is up to each of us to be as creative and gutsy as we can — willing to make life as profound as we can. The most radical spirituality is living as a free human being. And that freedom is ours to choose. Freedom cannot be bought. Freedom cannot be sold to us. Freedom doesn't come prepackaged. There is no right expression of this freedom. If in need of clarity about the wisdom or ignorance of an action, reflect: if what you are about to say or do will cause harm to yourself and or others, stop. On the other hand, if it elevates you and others, cultivate it.

We must be vigilant in our defense against indoctrination. Do not let anyone shape you in the image of his or her dogma. Don't even let teachers call you their student, unless that's what you want. Rather, be on equal footing, and learn from each other. There is no ultimate teaching to learn. Existence is the Dharma. Consciousness is the teacher. Life is the living art of finding and expressing liberation. There is no core philosophy that will free your mind. *Being free* frees the mind. Freedom is the only religion and it's where all true religions meet.

What fashions itself between spontaneous local beauty and the innate intelligence of the cosmos is the interrelated fabric of our social and political world. In order to discover the Dharma life that suits us, we must each come alive to the inner responsibility that our self as social and political being entails. This means opening our eyes to the world that surrounds us — from the inequities and misfortunes that force people to live on the streets of our neighborhoods to the blind logic of aggressive militarization that global powers are currently forcing upon distant nations and millions of innocent lives. We should not turn away from that suffering.

But witnessing is not enough. We must discover the conviction that declares the difference between right and wrong, the difference between status quo and making things better. It is our task, right now, to find the inner certainty and direction to commit our whole being to bringing about the best that natural freedom has to offer. There's no central plan of action for the next bold move. Let the mysterious constellation of the whole universe, inside and outside, be your guide, your guru, and your ultimate teacher.

ACKNOWLEDGMENTS

I wish to extend my deepest gratitude to my Dharma teachers, the Venerable Mahasi Sayadaw and Sayadaw U Pandita, for sharing the gift of their being and helping me to understand my own. This book rests firmly upon their shoulders. I would also like to express my respect and appreciation to my many friends in Burma, especially Aung San Suu Kyi, U Tin Oo, U Kyi Maung, and U Win Htein (who was rearrested in 1996 and is presently serving a fourteen-year sentence), for showing me that a "revolution of the spirit" means caring for things larger than oneself — struggling for the freedom of others as inseparable from one's own.

Among the key people in the West who made this book possible, most important was Jeannine Davies, whose tireless dedication to the Dharma, and support of the very best of me over the final five years it took to create this book, is something for which I will be forever grateful. Without her encouragement, kindness, and wisdom this book may not have come to fruition. My deep appreciation and indebtedness also goes to Jason Gardner, my editor at New World Library, who believed in me and this project from the very first moment he encountered my work. He did a superb job of editing and critiquing over the many phases of the book's development. I would also like to extend my love and deepest gratitude to Sharla Sava, for her friendship, editorial brilliance, and indefatigable support in helping me shape the World Dharma vision and articulate every page of this book.

I thank everyone at New World Library, especially Marc Allen, for their contributions toward bringing this book into the world. And finally, thanks to all the wonderful friends and folks who have attended my retreats, lectures, and spoken-word performances over the many years. Each of you has had a hand in helping me create this book.

I am indebted to everyone who helped, but all the errors and inconsistencies that may remain are my own. Although I have tried to remain as faithful to historical truth as possible, this book is based upon personal recollections gathered over several decades, and, as such, is bound by the limits of human fallibility.

INDEX

C

H

I

J

K

S

Y

Z

ABOUT THE AUTHOR

Photo credit: Robert Stefanowicz

Alan Clements was the first American to become a Buddhist monk in the Southeast Asian country of Burma. Clements lived there for many years in the seventies and eighties, including five years as a monk. During this time he trained in classical Buddhist psychology (*abhidharma*) and insight meditation (*vipassana*) with two of the most respected dharma masters of our era, the late Venerable Mahasi Sayadaw and his successor the Venerable Sayadaw U Pandita.

Since 1984, Clements has been an evocative spokesperson for the transformation of consciousness as the basis of freedom and dignity, lecturing and teaching hundreds of Dharma retreats in the United States, Canada, and Australia. His contemporary understanding of "essence spirituality" and its expression through spiritual activism have brought him international recognition.

Alan has lived in some of the most highly volatile areas of the world. In the jungles of Burma, in 1991, he was the first activist to witness and document the genocide of the ethnic minorities by the military dictatorship. He wrote about his observations in his first book, *Burma: The Next Killing Fields?* (Odonian Press, 1991). He then lived in the former Yugoslavia for nearly a year during the war, where he consulted with staff members of nongovernmental organizations and the United Nations on the "role of consciousness in regard to human rights, service, and activism."

In 1995, Clements made a risky journey back to Burma, where he coauthored *The Voice of Hope* (published in 1997 by Penguin in the United Kingdom, Seven Stories Press in the United States, and translated into thirteen languages), the internationally acclaimed book of conversations with Aung San Suu Kyi, 1991 Nobel Peace laureate and leader of her country's nonviolent struggle for freedom. In addition, Clements was the script revisionist and adviser for *Beyond Rangoon* (Castle Rock Entertainment, 1995) a feature film depicting Burma's struggle for democracy, directed by John Boorman.

Alan has been interviewed on ABC's *Nightline,* the *CBS Evening News, Voice of America,* BBC, and by *The New York Times, The London Times, Time, Newsweek, New Age Journal, Utne Reader,* and scores of other media worldwide.

◆

For information about Alan Clements's
other books and audio tapes, as well as his
retreat, lecture, and spoken-word performance schedule,
or to contact for speaking invitations, visit:
www.worlddharma.com

NEW WORLD LIBRARY is dedicated to publishing books and other media that inspire and challenge us to improve the quality of our lives and the world.

We are a socially and environmentally aware company, and we make every attempt to embody the ideals presented in our publications. We recognize that we have an ethical responsibility to our customers, our employees, and our planet.

We serve our customers by creating the finest publications possible on personal growth, creativity, spirituality, wellness, and other areas of emerging importance. We serve our employees with generous benefits, significant profit sharing, and constant encouragement to pursue our most expansive dreams. As members of the Green Press Initiative, we print an increasing number of books with soy-based ink on 100 percent postconsumer waste recycled paper. Also, we power our offices with solar energy and contribute to nonprofit organizations working to make the world a better place for us all.

Our products are available
in bookstores everywhere.
For our catalog, please contact:

New World Library
14 Pamaron Way
Novato, California 94949

Phone: 415-884-2100 or 800-972-6657
Catalog requests: Ext. 50
Orders: Ext. 52
Fax: 415-884-2199

Email: escort@newworldlibrary.com
Website: www.newworldlibrary.com